Newman and C

Newman and Conversion

Edited by
Ian Ker

T&T CLARK
EDINBURGH

T&T CLARK LTD
59 GEORGE STREET
EDINBURGH EH2 2LQ
SCOTLAND

First published 1997

ISBN 0 567 08553 8

British Library Cataloguing-in-Publication Data
A catalogue record for this book is available
from the British Library

Typeset by Fakenham Photosetting Ltd, Fakenham, Norfolk
Printed and bound in Great Britain by Biddles Ltd, Guildford

Contents

Introduction

Ian Ker

The conversion of John Henry Newman to the Church of Rome on 9 October 1845 was one of the most significant events in modern church history. The secession of the leader of the Oxford Movement from the Church of England not only signalled his own disillusion with the Tractarianism which he more than anyone else had been responsible for creating and propagating, but it also seemed to many to herald the end of the attempt to establish or re-establish the claim of the Anglican Church to be one of the three branches of the Church Catholic. Certainly the defection of the greatest theologian of the Church of England since Richard Hooker, and apart from John Wesley its most charismatic leader ever, has continued to haunt, even threaten successive generations of Anglicans.

From a larger perspective, Newman is easily the most important convert to Rome from the Churches of the Reformation. By contrast, the deeply Scriptural and Patristic theology that he brought into the Church of his adoption and which was so uncongenial to its authorities at the time can now be seen as the anticipation of the *ressourcement* or return to the sources of the tradition in the Bible and the Fathers that heralded in the twentieth century the Second Vatican Council.

Newman himself wrote much about the phenomenon of conversion. Not only did he tell the story of his own conversion in his *Apologia pro vita sua*, but the *Essay on the Development of Christian Doctrine*, which he wrote to test his growing convictions in favour of the claims of Rome, and which he also published in 1845, reflects too his view of the kind of personal development entailed in the growth that leads to individual conversion. His philosophical classic *An Essay in Aid of a Grammar of Assent* again explores the nature of assent that is involved in a religious conversion. And finally his two novels, *Loss and Gain* and *Callista*, are both on the theme of conversion.

In August 1995 an international conference was held at Oriel College, Oxford to mark the 150th anniversary of the reception of Newman into the Roman Catholic Church. Fr Michael Barber, SJ, the Bursar of Campion Hall, Oxford, conceived the idea and was largely responsible for the practical arrangements, particularly the remarkable liturgical celebrations. The actual organization was entrusted to the able hands of Mrs Priscilla Frost of Oxford Conference Management.

As academic director, I intended the conference to be interdisciplinary in the composition of its lectures and papers, thus interpreting the theme of conversion in the largest and widest sense. I also wanted well-known scholars, who were not necessarily Newman specialists, to contribute to the plenary lectures, from their own historical or literary or philosophical or theological perspectives. Of the contributions selected for this volume, all but one were plenary lectures. The one exception is that of Dr Ronald Begley, who was asked by me to enlarge his highly original seminar paper for inclusion in this collection.

Sheridan Gilley's wide-ranging paper emphasizes the cultural and religious importance within the English context of Newman's conversion, a conversion which has influenced so many other conversions, not least among writers, to whom Newman himself obviously speaks with special eloquence. Avery Dulles recounts the key stages in Newman's journey to Rome and reflects on its significance for the theology of conversion. Ian Ker points out that Newman had almost no experiential knowledge of the contemporary Church of his adoption, and describes how his post-conversion discovery of Catholicism affected the most intensely literary period of his life. Ronald Begley throws new light on an important passage relating to Newman's conversion in the *Apologia pro vita sua* by tracing its key metaphor to a passage in Virgil's *Aeneid*.

After these largely biographical, historical, and literary papers, there follows two essays of a philosophical nature. John Macquarrie explores the similarities and differences between Newman's and Kierkegaard's conceptions of the relation between faith and reason, both men being concerned to broaden a narrow rationalistic sense of reason to include the personal and the ethical. The views of Wittgenstein, especially the later Wittgenstein, on the rationality of belief are compared by Cyril Barrett with those of Newman, particularly with regard to the alleged circularity of the argument of the *Grammar of Assent*.

The year 1845 saw not only Newman's conversion but also the publication of his theological classic *An Essay on the Development of Christian Doctrine*, which he had deliberately set out to write in order to test his virtual certainty that the Church of England was in schism from the Catholic Church that was the heir to the primitive Apostolic Church. Aidan Nichols develops Newman's theory of development by complementing Newman's concept of the 'idea' of Christianity with Hans Urs von Balthasar's notion of the 'form' of revelation. In the final paper Terrence Merrigan contrasts Newman's remarkably positive analysis of natural religion in terms of conscience and conversion with both postmodern pluralist theology and the teaching of the Second Vatican Council on non-Christian religions.

I

Newman and the Convert Mind

Sheridan Gilley

There would have been converts to Roman Catholicism in England even without John Henry Newman. Most converts have been ordinary folk, converted by some sort of family connection, especially on their marriage to a practising Catholic.[1] Even on a more exalted intellectual level, the tradition of conversion among poets like Hopkins and Patmore goes back to the seventeenth century, to Crashaw and Dryden, and in Newman's own day, some of the most notable Catholic converts owed little enough to him. Thus the convert makers of the Romantic Gothic revival, Ambrose Phillipps de Lisle, Augustus Pugin and Kenelm Digby, were all received into the Church before Newman came to national prominence,[2] while there were some who felt the influence of another strong figure such as Henry Edward Manning. Yet Newman is Rome's great converter in England. His writings, above all the *Apologia,* and the glamour of his Anglican life in its Oxford setting, have contributed immeasurably to the modern English fascination with Rome; and through his books that 'most entrancing of voices, breaking the silence with words and thoughts which were a religious music – subtle, sweet, mournful'[3] still makes conversions to Rome today.

Thus one modern Roman convert, Muriel Spark, has written that 'if there is one comprehensive thing that can be said for Newman's writing, it is that he has a "voice"; it is his own and no one else's. To me, at least, it is a voice that never fails to start up, radioactive from the page, however musty the physical book.' Newman is supremely the thinker who taught that faith – and unfaith – are communicated by personal influence, as first by his Lord and Master, and he is the still-living embodiment of his own theory, for his voice conveys his person, a personality with an enchantment to the literary-minded like no other. Miss Spark declares that Newman 'is far less dead, to me, than many of my contemporaries; and less dead, even, than Socrates for whom, in the day-dreams of my young youth, I thought it would be lovely to lay down my life ... It was by way of Newman that I turned Roman Catholic. Not all the beheaded martyrs of Christendom, the ecstatic nuns of Europe, the five proofs of Aquinas, or the pamphlets of my Catholic acquaintance, provided anything like the answers that Newman did.'[4]

Although Miss Spark was born a Scot, with a Jewish father, she passed through an Anglo-Catholic phase, with a keen love of the King James Bible and Book of Common Prayer, and her words are characteristic of the way in which Anglican converts to Rome feel a special proprietorship in Newman, as their patron and prototype, the greatest of all those among them who have crossed the Tiber. Here is their own little story on an epic scale and with a proper hero, who, like them, was not born into the Catholic purple, but found the pearl of great price only after a long and arduous journey. In the phrases of Monsignor Ronald Knox, the convert who supremely inherited Newman's literary versatility and fastidiousness, Newman is the 'Great Auk' among Anglican converts, and his spiritual Odyssey or Aeneid is their own.[5]

Newman is, then, a representative figure, though his path to Rome is all his own. One important landmark on his intellectual pilgrimage is the *Lectures on the Prophetical Office* of 1837, the work in which he stands poised on the point of making the paradigm shift between Anglicanism and Roman Catholicism, by balancing an Anglican way of looking at things, in the credal essentials or fundamentals of the Episcopal Tradition, against the more generally Roman Catholic view which he calls the Prophetical Tradition, and which embraces the whole faith in the manner of the new Catholic Catechism. Newman's formal defence of his Roman conversion is his *Essay on the Development of Christian Doctrine*, which is in apologetic terms largely an answer to the Anglican objection to modern Rome that Rome is so unlike the Church of the early centuries. Yet for all its occasional passage of fine rhetoric in which the theme of the growth of Christian ideas and institutions reflects an underlying image of the growth in heart and mind of the individual believer, Newman's most personal, impassioned and accessible work remains the *Apologia*, the history of his religious opinions, that highly selective spiritual biography of which every reader knows the end before its beginning, and which might be retitled 'How I became a Roman Catholic'. The *Apologia* shows the inner life as a work of divine grace, but so binds grace to natural gracefulness as to seem to make the life a work of art.

This is partly why its influence has been strongest among converts with a literary calling or vocation like Miss Spark, who have come to Newman with an ear for his verbal music, and partly why the Catholic revival has been so much a literary affair, with a greater impact upon writers than among the scientists or businessmen who have no such notable Catholic convert model.

The Catholic convert mind is, then, more literary in the old belletrist sense than it is scientific or philosophical; though Newman's philosophy is important to it, as shall be shown. Even the work of the great convert scholars, like Edmund Bishop among liturgists and Christopher Dawson among historians, is marked by a kind of literary refinement traceable to Newman's influence. The literary dimension of conversion is demonstrated by Fr Stephen Brown's listing, of 1940, of more than three thousand novels in English by Catholics, at least half of them converts or the children or grandchildren of converts.[6] Minor convert novelists – Robert Hugh Benson, Maurice Baring, John Oliver Hobbes, John Ayscough, Sheila Kaye-Smith – were especially numerous. And among them is Newman, the author of two novels, both in different ways novels of conversion to Catholicism, *Loss and Gain* about conversion from Anglicanism and *Callista* about conversion from paganism.[7] This is where, despite all the magical resources of Dr David Newsome's own prose, itself not unmarked by Newman's influence, the comparison of Newman with his rival Manning must be to Newman's advantage, for Manning was not an original or creative thinker and did not write like an angel.[8] The Catholic Manning had two great practical universal ideals, the first on the challenge to faith, the second on the challenge to social order. Manning thought that an infallible Church and pope were the answer to the religious doubt of the age, and that the Church which championed social justice was the answer to its poverty. Thus his published literary output is both highly respectable and moving – his pamphlet 'The Child of the English Savage', a denunciation of cruelty to children, can still make the blood boil; but with the exception of *The Eternal Priesthood*, a book which needs to be republished, his work has hardly been reprinted in our century. His private and personal influence in his way and in his own day was just as great as Newman's, but as it belonged to the realm of deeds and to the spoken rather than the written word, so it died with those who had known him, whereas heart still speaks to heart wherever Newman finds readers.

Indeed Newman's influence is only confined by that of his printed medium, and has only suffered as young people, even middle-class ones, have deserted the culture of the printed book, though few can have ever, like the young A. N. Wilson, taken to Newman as other adolescents now take to drugs. But it was Newman who made the Catholic Church a power in the realm of all lovers of English prose, not merely of elegiac and poetic prose, but also of irony. No convert, not even Evelyn Waugh, can equal him in deadly, withering wit, and in satire sharper than a sword, though nothing seems to stop them trying. Wit, then, is one characteristic of the Catholic convert mind, and for that, Newman is in part responsible. The association has continued into our day; as one convert wrote upon another:

> Mary of Holyrood may smile indeed,
> Knowing what grim historic shade it shocks
> To see wit, laughter and the Popish creed
> Cluster and sparkle in the name of Knox.[9]

Aldous Huxley thought that Catholic converts matched their socks to the colours of the liturgical year, put on weight and wrote comic verse; the last at least is sometimes true, and Newman, who wrote the satirical novel *Loss and Gain* a few years after his conversion, and the delicious satire of the *Present Position of Catholics*, was the archetypal convert wit.[10] Indeed he is the only Catholic convert revolutionary in literature, with the possible exception of one figure he converted, Gerard Manley Hopkins, the fountain-head of modern English poetry. Otherwise Newman is perhaps the only intellectual convert revolutionary, again with one possible exception, Augustus Pugin, whom Newman rightly called a bigot, but who was a giant to architecture and architectural theory, and whose reputation lengthens with the years.

Newman's impact on Roman Catholic theology has also been enormous, but no one feels this quite as strongly as the Anglican convert, whose initial objection to Roman Catholicism has usually been that Rome was a papal and clerical tyranny which allowed no freedom of conscience, no freedom for the laity and no freedom for original theological thought. Newman made conscience the very foundation or fulcrum of his whole conception of religion; he argued for the right of the lay faithful to be consulted, albeit in a somewhat passive sense; and he expounded a constitutional conception of the Church, in which the institutional or regal element exercised by Rome was held in tension and balance by the priestly or devotional office of pastors and people and the prophetical or intellectual office of the theologians.

Manning thought that Newman was seeking to introduce 'the old Anglican, patristic, literary, Oxford tone'[11] into Roman Catholicism, and in a sense he was right, in that Newman was the Church of England's great gift to Catholic theology, his Catholic theology being the development and fulfilment of his theological work as an Anglican. His insistence on the continuities of his own life declares that a convert is someone who discovers he is wrong, but also in some profound sense that he is already right. Indeed as Newman argued himself in the *Lectures on Certain Difficulties Felt by Anglicans*, Rome was the proper destination of the Movement of 1833. Newman feared in turn that Manning's aggressive infallibilism was responsible for presenting to his countrymen those aspects of the Catholic Church most consonant with their prejudices against her, and that the definition of 1870 would inhibit Anglo-Catholic conversions. Peace be on both their ashes. There are Manning converts and Newman converts. Manning's militancy has appealed to one class of Anglican convert, in full flight from a Church which never knows its own mind;[12] but for many another, Newman has been a reassurance that creative thought and conscience are not incompatible with a proper Catholic loyalty, and that while the Church is a monarchy, she need not be a despotic one, but one with distributed and delegated powers. In this sense, Newman has done much to make the Catholic Church a more Anglican-convert-friendly place.

Yet while none would dispute Newman's influence on Catholic theology, he is much more powerful there, and as a literary figure, than in the world of non-Catholic British theology, where he is an isolated or token orthodox presence in a desert of liberal negation. He is not ignored by non-Catholic British theologians, but some of his principal themes – the role of the personal and the liturgical in acquiring and imparting religious knowledge, the development of doctrine, the non-propositional dimension of divine Revelation and the inadequacy of human reason and language to describe the infinite mystery of God – are put to liberal theological uses which he would himself have abhorred.

Thus Newman's demonstration of the historical elements in

the progressive definition of Christian doctrine, which neatly disposed of the Anglican appeal to a fixed or frozen antiquity, is taken by Anglican liberals to imply that all doctrine is relative, and that no final authority is to be accorded to the definitions of Nicaea or Chalcedon. The liberal understanding of the development of doctrine is that there was no doctrine worth developing. The non-propositional character of Revelation is liberally interpreted as declaring that Christianity is a religion so verbally evanescent or elusive that any generation can reshape it at will, while the idea that faith is personally and liturgically appropriated and communicated is made to mean that there can be as many systems of religious truth as there are persons and liturgies. And how often has that fateful sentence from the *Essay on the Development of Christian Doctrine*, 'to live is to change, and to be perfect is to have changed often',[13] been left without its introductory clauses, and twisted by knaves to make a trap for fools, who can be induced to think that any old change must be a step towards perfection?

There are, then, two ways of drinking Newman down, like drinking whiskey, neat, or with a liberal quantity of soda water. In my Anglican green and salad days, I was a consumer of liberal lashings of soda water. For there is an orthodox understanding of Newman, which takes him whole, and which sees in his personalism, individualism and apophaticism the necessary elements in an objective and apprehensible Catholicism; and from the era of Catholic Modernism, there has been the liberal mode of interpreting Newman, which takes him in part, which delights in his infinite suggestiveness and nuance, but which turns the very bulwarks and defences which he devised for orthodoxy into materials for an assault upon it.

This is where the literary Newman becomes the liberal Newman, and is a trap and a snare. The idea comes partly from the Ultramontane understanding of Newman as a 'Liberal Catholic'. The greatest of the mid-Victorian Liberal Catholics, Acton, saw that this was not so, even if it is granted that the Liberal Catholics were more Catholic than Liberal; and Newman had no thanks from either Acton or the Ultramontane William George Ward in his efforts to mediate between them.

But as Newman was not even a Liberal Catholic, so the non-Catholic or anti-Catholic liberal appropriation of Newman is even more of a misappropriation of the man whose life was a crusade against the influence of liberalism in religion. Not that

Newman was a conservative; rather, his commitment was to an orthodoxy transcending both liberalism and conservatism. Newman was never simply interested in preservationism because, while in certain circumstances it might protect the truth, the same could be said for bigotry and prejudice, and none of these was a sufficient answer to the wild living intellect of man. It was the challenge to the faith from the infidelity of his own day that moved Newman from Protestantism to Catholicism. It was Newman who, from his reading of Locke and Hume, demonstrated that unbelief enjoys no necessary intellectual preeminence over belief, which is just as reasonable a way of looking at the world, though it draws on different intellectual traditions, and first principles, and assumptions. And in his anti-liberalism, Newman unites a reason and a passion that reinforce each other in English pure and undefiled. 'The quality of his logic', wrote Chesterton of Newman, 'is that of a long but passionate patience, which waits until he has fixed all corners of an iron trap'[14] for the apostles of liberal irrationalism. He was, above all, anti-liberal in that his gaze was firmly fixed on God and not on man; or rather on God and on the man who is centred on God. Against the whole liberal man-centred view of things which dominates our day, and which is now so influential even in English religion, Newman sought, like Augustine and Calvin before him, the two things most necessary which all Christians must seek, the knowledge of God and of themselves.

And it is the Anglican convert who, by his own particular position, feels this most keenly. Newman is a hero to him because despite the thinnest of hides, he did not shrink from the duty of controversy. Newman knew from the Fathers of the early Church, and from his beloved Athanasius, that for all the human weaknesses to which it gives rise, controversy advances the cause of Christian truth. Though he did not like the battle, yet he fought. That 'subtle, sweet, mournful voice' had bite. He fought with wit and with passion. May God forgive those who forget Newman the controversialist, who flayed poor Kingsley alive, so that it was hardly a merit that Newman also forgave him. And he has the singular significance of having first defined the enemy. The Protestant objections to Rome are now mostly dead; on a range of traditionally Protestant issues, from prayer for the dead and arbitrary predestination to the merit of good works and the freedom of the will, the popular mind is papist and not Protestant. Even the old Protestant objection to priesthood is now recast in liberal form. The objections to Rome are now largely liberal ones, which tend to be as antipathetic to Protestantism as to Catholicism, indeed to any traditional form of Christianity.

For the sort of Protestantism which still maintains the mighty central Christian dogmas must look benign to Catholics beside the kind of liberalism which is the dissolution of all traditional Christian dogma, and which continues to alienate the more traditional type of Anglican, High or Low, or nothing in particular, through its steady advance within the Church of England. Here the drama of Newman's farewell to his Church in the loveliest and most haunted of its holy cities, Oxford, comes to the Anglican convert with a particular poignancy. For the convert has typically begun his religious life in a love affair with the Church of his baptism, and with an ardent desire to see her prosper. If of mildly romantic disposition, he rejoices in her imperial culture, in her ancient churches and cathedrals, in her choral tradition, in her great poets and her great divines, in her lay saints like Johnson and Gladstone, in the splendid cadences of the Prayer Book, and in the sense that here is the natural conjunction of being both English and Christian. Against this backdrop of English gentleness, and tolerance, and peace, Rome looks brisk and harsh and distinctly anti-national, un-English; if not an Italian Mission, then an Irish one. This Englishness has been part of the Church of England's appeal to such twentieth-century expatriates as the middle-European Sir Lewis Namier and the American T. S. Eliot, who felt that becoming Anglican was a normal and natural part of becoming English. Nor is this an unworthy motive, but like many a love affair, it may end in tears, if the liberal influence comes into conflict with the traditionalist temper and frame of mind in which the love affair was born.

Of course no Anglican becomes a Catholic simply by way of alienation from Anglicanism, but in conversion, there is push as well as pull, as a man moves to a more desirable house partly out of dissatisfaction with his own. Anglicans generally become unhappy with their Church when some Anglican bishop or divine denies the very faith that she has taught them, on a central doctrinal matter like the Virgin Birth or the Resurrection, or some aspect of the moral law; and as the modern Church of England is ever oscillating between periods and parties of orthodoxy and liberalism, so she is, by shifts and turns, in this time and that place under liberal control, ever surrendering her most loyal sons and daughters to bodies more orthodox than she.

Of course Newman did not slay the liberal hydra, either within the Church of England or outside it, but he showed how it could be opposed, on its own ground and with its own weapons. When Newman defined liberalism as 'the anti-dogmatic principle', he meant the anti-Christian anti-dogmatic principle, for he went on to define a range of liberal dogmas, and thereby fathered Chesterton's fundamental conviction that there are only two kinds of people, 'those who accept dogmas and know it and those who accept dogmas and don't know it'.[15] For Newman saw that there is no dogma more binding than liberal dogma, no view more deeply founded than the liberal view on unexamined pre-conception and prejudice, and so he was among the first to foresee and to oppose that liberal dechristianization of the Church of England which has been part of the dechristianization of England. In that he is a hero to all those Anglican converts to Rome who in much humbler measure have tried to do the same, and then given up the task as hopeless.

The liberal reaction tried to take over Newman as it has sought to take over everything, even in his own day, as in the seculariz-ation of Newman's faith into Matthew Arnold's conception of religion as 'morality touched by emotion' and an aesthetic of 'sweetness and light', while the transformation of Newman into Walter Pater's 'hard gem-like flame' is a subject almost as morally depressing, as is the twentieth-century substitution, now being deconstructed, of the religion of literature for a living faith. Of course, even a liberal Newman keeps alive among liberals ideas which would otherwise die for want of nourishment, and which lie lurking like good angels in some robber's cave to lead a man into a better way. More flies are caught with honey than with vinegar, and the beautiful can be the path to truth. Newman him-self united the moral power of the Hebrew with the grace of the Hellene; but he also ridiculed aestheticism as dandyism, and a merely aesthetic interest in him is to be sharply distinguished from a moral one. Newman's first love and final architectural preference was for the neo-classical Trinity College Chapel, and he was never very sympathetic to that Gothic Catholic convert frame of mind, born out of a passion for the middle ages and all their works, which reached its apotheosis in the splendid extrava-gances of John Patrick Crichton-Stuart, third Marquess of Bute. Indeed Newman was authentically Victorian as well as Catholic in his instinctive hostility to the idea of art for art's sake, the bat-tle cry of the late Victorian reaction against Victorianism. Hence his withering remarks in *The Tamworth Reading Room* on the powerlessness of a purely philosophical or literary religion; and so the work about Newman which most completely misunderstands him is G. Egner's *Apologia pro Charles Kingsley*, which misrepresents the mind in the *Grammar of Assent* as arbitrarily choosing its beliefs according to its aesthetic preference for one set of images over another.[16] For as Newman insisted, faith is not aesthetics, or philosophy, or knowledge; as one Anglican convert to Catholicism put it of his conversion:

> The sages have a hundred maps to give
> That trace their crawling cosmos like a tree,
> They rattle reason out through many a sieve
> That stores the sand and lets the gold go free;
> And all these things are less than dust to me
> Because my name is Lazarus and I live.[17]

Yet faith is knowledge of a kind. It is notable that Miss Spark came to Newman not through aestheticism, but as one wanting answers; and wanting answers from religion, especially God-given ones, is, to modern liberals, the cardinal sin. The bishop in C. S. Lewis's *The Great Divorce* prefers his Theological Discussion Society in Hell, which considers all questions open, to Heaven, where there will be only answers.[18] So, too, the main interest in Miss Spark's work, as Leon Litvack makes clear in his excellent article on the subject, lies in her fascination with the moral opacity of human nature, a mystery almost as great as the ultimate divine mystery. But to Spark it was Newman who supremely tried to make the moral darkness day, as he looked into himself. It was, above all, Newman's sincerity that attracted her, his ruthlessness about himself: 'He was sincere as light: "Every thought I think is a thought, and every word I write is writing" ',[19] as he set out to make clear, in words of utter clarity and simplicity, that most treacherous of all knowledge, the moral self-knowledge by which man either lives or dies.

That quest for self-knowledge is part of the mental condition of the convert: how can I be sure of what I must believe? How can I know that I am right? Newman offers an argued assurance that the believer can know, that he can be certain, without any moral treason to himself; that the subjective quest for certitude in matters of religion, the very certitude to which the liberal declares that no one has a right, can look to the eternal order of things and find there a response. The philosophical demonstration of the right, the reasonable right, the conscientious right in right reason, to certitude is, of course, the *Grammar of Assent*, with its argument that there is nothing unreasonable about believing what, in one sense, cannot be wholly proven and, in another, cannot be wholly understood. But Newman declared in his Anglican sermon on 'The Testimony of Conscience':

> Now, I suppose, absolute certainty about our state cannot be attained at all in this life: but the nearest approach to such certainty, which is possible, would seem to be afforded by this consciousness of openness and singleness of mind, this good understanding ... between the soul and its conscience, to which St. Paul so often alludes. 'Our rejoicing is this', he says, 'the testimony of our conscience, that in simplicity and godly sincerity we have had our conversation in the world.' He did not rejoice in his faith, but he was justified by faith, because he could rejoice in his sincerity.[20]

So much is this the case that Newman argues that the individual in such a condition 'is accepted *in* that state in which he is, be it ... heathenism, schism, superstition, or heresy; and that, because his faults and errors *at present* are not wilful'.[21] He is as sincere as he can possibly be.

It may seem odd to fasten on sincerity as a touchstone of Newman's appeal to the convert. As a moral category, sincerity has been employed by liberals to declare the superiority of the subjective, the individual and the personal over the objective, the collective and the authoritative, from the archetypal Latitudinarian Anglican Bishop, Benjamin Hoadly, never mentioned by Newman without a snap or a sigh, to J. D. Salinger in *The Catcher in the Rye*; it does not matter what one believes as long as one is sincere about it. Newman's sincerity was partly his literary art; he was 'absolutely himself in his power of writing',[22] and as Gerard Manley Hopkins himself said, 'his tradition is that of cultured, the most highly educated, conversation, ... [which] gives it a charm of unaffected and personal sincerity which nothing else could'.[23] But in Newman the duty of sincerity is also an awesome thing, not easily or lightly achieved, being the inner character of the soul, whatever its beliefs, which is hungering and thirsting after righteousness; which is utterly resolved to do its best to find the truth and to obey it. For sincerity arises for Newman from the sovereign conscience, an endowment of human nature which is ultimately revealed as the channel of the divine grace which has prompted it to life from the first, the pope within, the aboriginal Vicar of Christ, the very voice of God. And conscience is the origin of sincerity, which in turn is the author of conversion.

Thus sincerity is linked in Newman to a whole range of themes belonging to the darker or severer side of his religion. There is a liberal tendency to deprecate these aspects of Newman's Anglican preaching, like so much Evangelical preaching of its time, the constant call to seriousness and holiness, the nearness of Hell, death and judgement, the worry as to the likely fewness of the elect, the unrelenting moralism, the demand for the Law's stern fires and a perpetual Ash Wednesday, which is hardly a balanced view of the Christian Year. But while Newman outgrew too one-sided an emphasis on these things, the thirst for moral and spiritual truth for Newman is rooted in this primal moral sense, and without this longing for righteousness no one would ever be properly converted to anything.

This longing has its links to the affections and the imagination, but it is to be rigidly distinguished from them. Newman learned from his Evangelical mentor, Thomas Scott, that conversion moves the mind even as it touches the heart, and it brings, not the freedom from the moral law beloved by Calvinist antinomians, but the power to obey it. Newman came to reject Evangelicalism in part because he thought it overstressed certain sorts of spiritual excitement, especially in an emphasis on sudden conversion, at the expense of the moral. Christ appealed, Newman preached, not to the excited affections for conversion, but to conscience; for conscience is the true root of faith as a lasting principle, and is therefore the fit foundation of another lasting principle, the spiritual mind, which is also properly considered the truly philosophical mind, and not just the heart. Newman's philosophy can be called either moralism or personalism. His interest in what creates character and the moral life derives from his first Evangelical conviction of sin, and those who dislike this element in Newman must simply dislike Christianity, because this is a part of any Christianity deserving the name. The greatest of the English literary converts after Newman was Chesterton, who came to the Church 'to restore his innocence',[24] asking for absolution from sin. This is no more than the New Testament teaching in which conversion is above all else *metanoia*, repentance. None of this is very attractive to the modern liberal temperament, but as Chesterton remarks, we need the Church to tell us when we are wrong, not when we are right, and as Newman declares, the fashionable religion of the day, which shies away from conscience, sin, death and judgement, is merely the religion of this passing world.

All this, then, is in a good sense Evangelical, for Newman was an Evangelical convert before he was a Roman Catholic one; he had two conversions, one Protestant, and one Catholic. His Protestant conversion, in 1816 when he was fifteen, might be called in neo-scholastic fashion his conversion to a *fides qua creditur*, in the individual act of faith, by which every believer believes; while his Catholic conversion in 1845 might be defined as the *fides quae creditur*, the collective fullness of the faith which is believed, that whole body of belief which is the Church's faith, and in which even the devils believe and tremble. The first conversion was, by his own account, primary to the whole of the rest of his life; and without his primitive consciousness of himself and his Creator he would hardly have become a Catholic. Of course he rejected much of his Evangelical phase: Lutheran justification by faith alone, Calvinist final perseverance, and above all what followed from this, the Evangelical insistence on seeing everyone in morally black and white terms as all saint or sinner. Miss Spark loves Newman's moral subtlety, his delight in the nuance of personality. Yet it was a blessing that he encountered Protestantism in its most intellectually hard-headed form, the religion of John Calvin, the only form of Protestantism which can hold a candle for precision and self-coherence to Roman Catholicism. For all his later reservations about calling that first conversion 'Evangelical', Newman was the principal if not the only means by which the great English Evangelical tradition, the tradition of Baxter and Bunyan, passed into Roman Catholicism, so that the once converted might be converted yet again.

For a convert is someone who has passed through water and fire. He is twice-born. His decision is a matter of life and death. To feel the force of the great rhetorical conclusion to the *Essay on the Development of Christian Doctrine*, with its refrain that 'time is short, eternity is long', one needs to undergo something of the experience of conversion behind it. But its theme is to consider its argument, not to dismiss it as the result of mere emotion, even while the passage conveys the very passion it denies. Conversion comes with tears, and sorrow, as well as joy; Newman is the poet of both moods, even while his perfect self-restraint intensifies the emotion in the very act of expressing it, and so saves himself, with that wonderful English reserve which is again supremely his, from the indecency of too public an emotional display.

Now it is perfectly possible to read Newman and ignore his stern moralism; but it is here, supremely, that Newman speaks to the convert mind, even more in what he writes of the individual act of faith than in the faith to be believed. No one is converted either to Catholicism or to Christianity by the literary Newman, by the spiritual beauties of Newman, bound up in some limp Victorian purple leather volume, but by the moral Newman, the Augustinian Newman, the Evangelical Newman; it is in his stern unbending call to sincerity and seriousness that Newman is the master of the convert mind.

Last, he is master of that mind in his desire for inclusiveness and continuity. As early as the second of his *University Sermons*, he had come to the idea that Christianity must contain whatever is true in other religions within itself; that Catholicism is the completion and fulfilment of all those other aspirations to the good and true which otherwise wander forlorn throughout the world. Thus Newman thought that in becoming a Catholic, he was going from a smaller house into a larger one. The Church is greater than the world to which it ministers, and so the convert is always conscious of an inferiority, like Ronald Knox's response to an Irish priest's offer of a triple measure of whiskey: 'Whoa! I'm only a convert'.[25] The Catholic convert is an heir, not by birth but by adoption. Like the Magi of the famous prayer in Evelyn Waugh's *Helena*, he has come late into the kingdom. But Newman's undying love for his old Anglican friends, Keble and Pusey above all, and his continuing solicitude for Anglicans, which please God still continues, may lead the convert to hope that there is a place for four centuries of Anglican thought and achievement in full communion with Peter, in the Universal Church. A recent distinguished Anglican convert to Rome remarked that he waited for more than an hour for the priest to say to him what he had to hear: that in becoming a Catholic, he left no true and valuable part of his Anglican heritage behind him. Yet the convert must also see, as Newman did, that Catholicism is richer than his much-prized Anglican inheritance. A modern Catholic convert, George Marshall, in his study of Edwin Muir, who never formally entered the Church of Rome, has described how Muir was overwhelmed in a church in Rome by the Incarnational principle in an image of the Annunciation: 'I discovered in Italy that Christ had walked on earth'. This accompanied the sense that the Bible and sermon-centred Scottish Calvinism of Muir's youth had turned the Word made flesh back into a religion of words. 'The Word made flesh is here made word again.'[26] Newman always distrusted 'unreal words';[27] but his real words had always the aspiration to truth. There are many roads to Rome, and some only travel a part of the journey; but Newman was sure that all roads lead there.

Notes

1. Pauline Ann Adams, *Converts to the Roman Catholic Church in England c 1830–1870* (unpublished B.Litt. thesis, University of Oxford, 1977). On the statistical patterns of conversion to Catholicism in Britain in the twentieth century, see Robert Currie, Alan Gilbert, Lee Horsley, *Churches and Churchgoers: Patterns of Church Growth in the British Isles since 1700* (Oxford, 1977), pp. 30, 61.

2. Digby was received in 1824, de Lisle in 1825, and Pugin, according to the best authority, in June 1835 (Phoebe Stanton, *Pugin* (London, 1971), p. 10). The eminent named converts are listed in W. Gordon Gorman, *Converts to Rome* (London, 1910), which is dedicated to the 'Heralds of the New Spring', all pre-Newman converts, Henry Digby Best, Kenelm Digby, de Lisle, and Fr George Ignatius Spencer.

3. Matthew Arnold, quoted in Basil Willey, *Nineteenth-Century Studies: Coleridge to Matthew Arnold* (London, 1964), p. 82.

4. Muriel Spark, Foreword, in Vincent F. Blehl (ed.), *Realizations: Newman's own Selection of his Sermons* (London, 1964), pp. v–ix; cited in Leon Litvack, 'The Road to Rome: Muriel Spark, Newman and the Nevertheless Principle', in David Bevan (ed.), *Literature and the Bible* (Atlanta, Georgia, 1993), pp. 31–2.

5. Ronald Knox, *Barchester Pilgrimage* (London, 1938), p. 82; Ronald Knox, *A Spiritual Aeneid* (London, 1918; edition of 1958).

6. Stephen J. Brown, SJ, *Novels and Tales by Catholic Writers* (Dublin, 1940). There is also a listing of Catholic biographies by Fr Stephen Brown, *An Index of Catholic Biographies* (Dublin, 1930).

7. Alan G. Hill, 'Originality and Realism in Newman's Novels', in Ian Ker and Alan G. Hill (eds), *Newman after a Hundred Years* (Oxford, 1990), pp. 21–42.

8. David Newsome, *The Convert Cardinals: John Henry Newman and Henry Edward Manning* (London, 1993).

9. Evelyn Waugh, *The Life of the Right Reverend Ronald Knox* (London, 1959), p. 199.

10. Ian Ker, 'Newman the Satirist' in Ker and Hill (eds), *Newman after a Hundred Years* (Oxford, 1990), pp. 1–20.

11. J. Derek Holmes, *More Roman than Rome: English Catholicism in the Nineteenth Century* (London and Shepherdstown, 1978), p. 127.

12. Thus Knox: 'I came into the Church, it seems to me, in a white heat of orthodoxy, Manning's disciple rather than Newman's; and when I took the anti-modernist oath, it was something of a disappointment that the Vicar-General was not there to witness the fervour I put into it – he had gone out to order tea.' *A Spiritual Aeneid*, p. xx.

13. *An Essay on the Development of Christian Doctrine* (London, 1845), p. 39: 'It changes . . . in order to remain the same. In a higher world it is otherwise, but here below to live is to change, and to be perfect is to have changed often.'

14. G. K. Chesterton, *The Victorian Age in Literature* (London, 1908), p. 48.

15. Maisie Ward, *Gilbert Keith Chesterton* (London, 1944), p. 189.

16. G. Egner, *Apologia pro Charles Kingsley* (London, 1969).

17. G. K. Chesterton, 'The Convert', *Collected Poems* (London, 1927), p. 84.

18. C. S. Lewis, *The Great Divorce: A Dream* (London, 1945), pp. 40, 42.

19. Foreword to *Realizations*, cited Litvack, p. 45.

20. *Parochial Sermons* (London, 1840), vol. V, p. 285.

21. *Ibid.*, p. 287.

22. Anne Mozley, *Letters and Correspondence of John Henry Newman*, 2 vols (London, 1891), vol. I, p. 9; cited in Walter E. Houghton, *The Art of Newman's* Apologia (New Haven, 1945), p. 71.
23. C. C. Abbott (ed.), *Further Letters of Gerard Manley Hopkins* (London, 1938), p. 232; cited in Houghton, *loc cit.*
24. Maisie Ward, p. 396.
25. Penelope Fitzgerald, *The Knox Brothers* (London, 1977), p. 177.
26. George Marshall, *In a Distant Isle: The Orkney Background of Edwin Muir* (Edinburgh, 1987), pp. 124–7.
27. 'Unreal Words', *Parochial Sermons*, vol. V, pp. 33–52.

2

Newman: The Anatomy of a Conversion

Avery Dulles, SJ

Reflecting on his own religious pilgrimage, John Henry Newman in the *Apologia pro vita sua* formulated the principle that the mind ascends by a consistent process from its first to its final religious idea, so that the reason why one assents to any religious truth can become the reason for assenting to the whole Catholic faith. In true philosophy, Newman maintained, there is no medium between atheism and Catholicity. In other words, a perfectly consistent mind would have to embrace either the one or the other of these alternatives. Reversing the principle, Newman also held that the reason for denying any one article of Catholic faith, carried to its logical conclusion, would be a reason for rejecting each and every religious truth.[1]

This principle, as Newman acknowledged, could easily be interpreted as if it meant that if one is not a Catholic one must be a virtual atheist, but it can also be interpreted more benignly to say that anyone who is not an atheist, and who sincerely adheres to any religious truth at all, is already reaching forward to the fullness that is professed in Catholic Christianity.[2] All intermediate positions, such as the Protestant and the Anglican, contain a chiaroscuro of affirmation and rejection that makes for ambiguity. Their members are caught in a web of belief and unbelief, so that to be logical they must either rise higher or descend to a lower and more consistent position.

Although Newman recognized the possibility of a descent as well as an ascent, the term 'conversion', for him, applied only to the latter. As he wrote in *Tracts for the Times*, No. 85, the religious mind is drawn from error to truth 'not by losing what it had, but by gaining what it had not. .... True conversion is ever of a positive, not a negative character.'[3] Indeed it seemed problematic to Newman whether the term 'conversion' was appropriate to his own religious pilgrimage, since he had never undergone a violent change or reversal of views, such as was described in the writings of the Evangelicals. Regarding his adolescent acceptance of the gospel, he wrote in his journal:

> I speak of conversion with great diffidence, being obliged to adopt the language of books. For my feelings, so far as I can remember, were so different from any account I have ever read, that I dare not go by what may be an individual case.[4]

And again:

> In the matter in question, viz. conversion, my own feelings were *not* violent, but a returning to, a renewing of, principles, under the power of the Holy Spirit, which I already felt, and in a measure acted on, when young.[5]

This is not to deny that conversion, even in Newman's case, did involve the renunciation of certain beliefs that were formerly held. But he regarded such expendable beliefs as having been, from the beginning, only secondary and superficial; they could not have been certitudes, he held, for certitude, by its very nature, is irreversible.[6]

The logic of the movement from one position to the next, according to Newman, is not merely syllogistic or propositional. It is fed by concrete experiences involving the emotions and the imagination. The heart as well as the head must be drawn. Usually the affections precede but, at least in Newman's own case, the process did not come to completion without rational confirmation. Charles Reding seems to speak for Newman when in the novel *Loss and Gain* he exclaims 'I know where my heart is! But I must go by reason.'[7] The kind of reason Newman had in mind was an exercise of that practical or prudential intelligence that forms the central theme of his great epistemological treatise, the *Grammar of Assent.*

In his celebrated letters regarding the Tamworth Reading Room (1841), Newman gave a first sketch of the kind of logic that he saw involved in religious conversion. The deductions of science, he maintained, have no power of persuasion.

> The heart is commonly reached, not through the reason, but through the imagination, by means of direct impressions, by the

testimony of facts and events, by history, by description. Persons influence us, voices melt us, looks subdue us, deeds inflame us.[8]

As we shall see, personal contacts were crucially important in the evolution of Newman's religious views.

Because the operation of the illative sense involves the whole person, it inevitably takes time. In a sermon on 'Sudden Conversions' Newman explains: 'When men change their religious opinions really and truly, it is not merely their opinions that they change, but their hearts; and this evidently is not done in a moment – it is slow work.'[9] Applying this principle to his own case, he wrote in the *Apologia*:

> All the logic in the world would not have made me move faster towards Rome than I did; as well might you say that I have arrived at the end of my journey, because I see the village church before me, as venture to assert that the miles, over which my soul had to pass before it got to Rome, could be annihilated, even though I had had some far clearer vision than I then had, that Rome was my ultimate destination. Great acts take time.[10]

For all that, religious conversion for Newman was not a mere process of discovery. Although private judgement must be exercised in the approach to faith, the act of faith itself is anything but a product of one's own reason. It is a total submission of one's mind and heart to the word of God as it comes through a duly commissioned herald, which, for Newman as a Catholic, meant the living voice of the divinely commissioned Church.[11]

Keenly sensitive to the personal element in religious conviction, Newman was reluctant to construct a general theory of conversion. 'In religious inquiry', he asserted, 'each of us can speak only for himself, and for himself he has a right to speak.' In this sphere, therefore, 'egotism is true modesty'.[12] Reflecting on his own progress towards Catholic faith, he interpreted it as an ascending movement in which he had made advances in order to avoid receding to a lower level. In his religious journey he encountered a series of challenges that impelled him to believe more in order not to renounce what he already believed.

The Point of Departure

As the point of departure for his spiritual pilgrimage Newman looked back to the spontaneous religiosity of his childhood years. Even before he formed any clear religious convictions, he recalls, his imagination dwelt on an unseen world inhabited by spirits who possessed magical powers. In his early years, he says, he was very superstitious and used to sign himself with the cross before going into the dark.[13]

The religion of the child, according to Newman, has strong moral overtones. One can easily sense the autobiographical background of Newman's description of the sentiments he attributes to the lad of five or six:

> The child clearly understands that there is a difference between right and wrong; and when he has done what he believes is wrong, he is conscious that he is offending One to whom he is amenable, whom he does not see, who sees him. His mind reaches forward with a strong presentiment to the thought of a Moral Governor, sovereign over him, mindful and just. It comes to him like an impulse of nature to entertain it.[14]

This spontaneous childhood faith was nourished in Newman's case by that kind of 'Bible religion' that he characterized in his *Grammar of Assent* as 'the national religion of England'. The practice of reading the Bible in public and in private, he there states, has attuned the minds of the citizens to religious thoughts, even though it does not, in most cases, lead to anything deeper than a merely 'notional' assent to religious truth.[15]

In the Newman household such biblical religion was strongly inculcated. 'I was brought up from a child to take great delight in reading the Bible', he writes, and adds: 'Of course I had perfect knowledge of my Catechism.'[16] Among the benefits of Bible religion Newman reckons the high moral standard it imparts. This was true in his own case. The Bible and the catechism confirmed Newman's spontaneous inclination to accept the reality of a personal God who is the supreme lawgiver and omniscient judge of our most secret thoughts and acts.

First Conversion

Newman's tranquil belief was troubled when at the age of fourteen he read several works by eighteenth-century unbelievers. Among these were Thomas Paine's tracts against the Old Testament, David Hume's critique of belief in miracles, and some French poems, perhaps by Voltaire, denying the immortality of the soul.[17] In order for Newman's superficial biblical religion to escape destruction by these challenges, it would have to be transformed into something stronger.

The reinforcement, in Newman's case, came from a teacher of classics at his school, the Reverend Walter Mayers, a Calvinist Evangelical. But John, unlike his younger brother Francis, who embraced Evangelicalism at the age of eleven, held out for some time. He raised objections against Mayers based on Pope's *Essay on Man*, which proposed an ethic of virtue without recourse to divine help.[18]

Mayers put in Newman's hands a number of Calvinist books that settled his doubts and gave new clarity to his religious vision. One such work, written by William Romaine, probably confirmed him in his previous sense of God's immediate and special providence over him as an individual. This solitary religion is reflected in one of Newman's early sermons on the immortality of the soul:

> To understand that we have souls, is to feel our separation from things visible, our independence of them, our distinct existence in ourselves, our individuality, our power of acting for ourselves this way or that way, our accountableness for what we do. These are the great truths which lie wrapped up indeed in a child's mind, and which God's grace can unfold in spite of the influence of the external world; but at first this outward world prevails.[19]

Newman's growing consciousness of God's immediate presence gradually dispelled every temptation to atheism, deism, and autonomous humanism. It convinced him that there were but two luminously self-evident beings, the self and the Creator. His sense of accountability to God made it easy for him to accept Christian teaching on life beyond the grave.

Among the books recommended by Mayers the one that chiefly influenced Newman was the spiritual autobiography of another Evangelical, Thomas Scott, entitled *The Force of Truth*. Describing his own progress from Unitarianism to Trinitarianism, Scott impressed on Newman a keen sense of dogma. Before he was sixteen Newman, making use of this and other books, drew up a list of biblical texts in support of each verse of the Athanasian creed.[20] Throughout life he was to make use of certain aphorisms from Scott, such as 'holiness before peace' and 'growth is the only evidence of life'.[21]

Newman picked up at this time several beliefs that he would later have to reject. One of these was the Calvinist doctrine, taught in rigorous form by Romaine, that conversion was an infallible sign of final election.[22] From a certain Thomas Newton he absorbed the idea that the pope was the Antichrist predicted in certain biblical prophecies. This prejudice, which continued to trouble him for the next twenty years, was partly offset by Joseph Milner's five-volume *History of the Church of Christ*, a work enriched with lengthy quotations from Latin Fathers such as Ambrose and Augustine, kindling Newman's lifelong passion for patristic literature. The tension between Protestant biblicism and Anglican devotion to the Fathers produced in Newman a kind of mental unrest that was to work itself out in future years.

To summarize the end-result of this first crisis, we may say that Newman was able to meet the challenge of Enlightenment rationalism thanks to the personal influence of Mayers and the reading of authors such as Romaine and Scott. Moving beyond the naivety of his childhood fantasies and the empty formalism of biblical religion, he achieved a real assent to the immediate presence of God and a sincere submission to the teaching of Scripture and the ancient creeds. Although he did not spell out the grounds for this conversion, he seems to have relied on his own spiritual intuitions, the personal example of convinced believers, and the logical coherence between biblical and ecclesiastical teaching. In advancing towards his new position he did not renounce, but rather confirmed, his own previous intimations of a higher world and his devotion to Scripture. By the age of sixteen Newman had become attached to the Evangelical wing of the Church of England.

Second Conversion

After his ordination in 1824, at the age of twenty-three, Newman performed two years of parochial work as curate at St Clement's, while continuing his scholarly and academic work at Oxford. During this period he distanced himself from the Calvinist and Evangelical features of his earlier conversion, finding that they did not correspond either with his own experience or with the realities of parish ministry. It might have been expected that, as he left what he called 'the crags and precipices of Luther and Calvin', he might 'take refuge in the flats' of a dry, naturalistic theology, Arminian and Latitudinarian in character.[23] Prodded by keen logicians such as Richard Whately, he began to feel a certain disdain for antiquity and to indulge in flippant language about the Fathers. In the *Apologia* he confesses: 'I was beginning to prefer intellectual excellence to moral; I was drifting in the direction of the Liberalism of the day.'[24]

Just as he previously had to resist the solicitations of eighteenth-century deism, so now Newman had to take a position with reference to positivism, empiricism, and utilitarianism or, more generally, to the anti-dogmatic spirit in religion that he identified with liberalism. The 'broad church' party in the Church of England inherited the spirit of seventeenth-century Latitudinarianism. It emphasized what could be known of God by natural reason, was impatient of mystery, and tended to treat dogma as mere opinion. The Evangelical party of the Church was no help in the struggle against liberalism, for the Evangelicals were themselves anti-dogmatic. They seemed to have lost the simplicity and unworldliness that Newman admired in Scott and Milner. By their emotional approach to faith, and their privileging of the heart over the head, the Evangelicals played into the hands of the liberals, who denied that any true and objective knowledge could be derived from revelation.

To meet the threat that liberalism posed to his own faith and that of the Church, Newman had to look further. Again a providential encounter set him on the right track. In the *Apologia* he speaks of his early meetings with John Keble as of an encounter with a living saint. Keble's *The Christian Year*, a volume of poems accompanying the Sundays and Feast Days of the liturgical cycle, appeared in 1827, and made a deep impression upon him. The book struck an original note, he said, and produced new music, long unheard in England.

Newman's association with Keble confirmed him in two crucial insights, both congenial to his temperament. One was that material phenomena are types and instruments of unseen realities of a higher order. This conviction disposed him to gain a greater appreciation of the sacraments, of the mysterious element in revelation, and of the communion of the saints. The second key intuition was that certitude is achieved not simply by the force of the evidence that prepares us to assent to the divine, but by the living power of the faith and love with which we assent.[25]

Together with John Keble, Edward Pusey, and Hurrell Froude, Newman became a leader of the Anglo-Catholic party at Oxford and the chief author of a series of pamphlets called *Tracts for the Times*. The Tractarian movement was founded on distinctly anti-Protestant principles, which Newman deemed necessary to resist the inroads of liberal rationalism. Among these principles were the authority of apostolic tradition, the apostolic succession in the ministry, baptismal regeneration, the visibility of the Church, and the independence of the Church from the State. In this period Newman retained and even strengthened some of his earlier convictions, including his high moral standards, his dogmatic Trinitarian faith, and his devotion to the early Fathers. But he felt it necessary to abandon his Calvinist views on the sufficiency of Scripture, on justification by faith, and on the indefectibility of grace.

Fundamental to Anglo-Catholicism were the tenets that the Church of Christ must exist visibly in the world today, and that it must be both Catholic and apostolic. To defend these tenets against objections coming respectively from the Protestant and Roman sides, Newman and his colleagues maintained that the Catholic Church had three branches: Orthodox, Roman, and Anglican, all of them stemming from the undivided Church of the first centuries. In relation to Roman Catholicism and Protestantism, Anglicanism represented a middle path, a *via media*, avoiding the errors of the two extremes. Protestants, with their biblicism, fell short of recognising the full content of faith as formulated in the creeds and dogmas of the early councils. Roman Catholics, by contrast, had overlaid the pure doctrine of the ancient Church with accretions that had no basis in Scripture or early tradition. Thus the Anglican communion, while not lacking Catholicity, could regard itself as the one in which the mark of apostolicity was most perfectly verified.

Although Newman's transition from Anglican Evangelicalism to Anglo-Catholicism is not commonly called a conversion, it does show the same basic features as his original move to Evangelical Christianity and his later passage to Roman Catholicism. In this second conversion he carried with him his earlier convictions regarding the unseen presence of God, his own moral accountability to the divine lawgiver, and the Trinitarian and Christological dogmas of antiquity. He fought off the challenge of liberalism by interpreting the Anglican tradition in a Catholic sense. In so doing he shuffled off certain Calvinist doctrines that had never been central to his thinking. With the help of devout friends such as Keble, Pusey, and Froude, he was able to embrace the Anglicanism of the Thirty-Nine Articles, interpreting them in a Catholic sense. To all appearances Newman had reached his definitive position.

Third Conversion

The viability of Anglo-Catholicism depended on the Catholic interpretation of the beliefs and polity of the Church of England. In the years between 1839 and 1843 Newman's adherence to this interpretation was shaken by a series of unexpected blows.

One set of challenges arose from his research in patristic history. Even if the Anglican Church was apostolic, he wondered, could it rightly claim to be Catholic? Doubts were first implanted in his mind in the summer of 1839, when he read an article by Cardinal Nicholas Wiseman in the *Dublin Review* comparing the position of the Anglicans of the day with that of the Donatists in Africa at the time of Augustine. In that article Newman came across the dictum of Augustine, '*securus judicat orbis terrarum* (the whole world judges surely)'. These words struck Newman with a power that he had never felt from any words before. They kept ringing in his ears. He could not deny that the deliberate judgement of the whole Church is a final sentence against such portions of it as protest and secede.[26]

Reflecting more deeply on the lessons of history, Newman began to see the Church of England as in a situation analogous to that of ancient dissident groups such as the Semi-Arians of the fourth century and the moderate Eutychians (or Monophysites) of the fifth. In these conflicts, he noted, truth lay not with the mediating parties but with Rome, which stood at one extreme. Why, then, could the truth not lie with the Catholics against the Anglicans today? What assurance could the *via media* proffer?

As he struggled in vain to assure himself that the Anglican Church was, after all, Catholic, several new occurrences conspired to disillusion him. One was the rejection by the Anglican bishops of Tract 90, in which Newman sought to defend his Catholic interpretation of the Thirty-Nine Articles. On top of this came the affair of the Jerusalem bishopric. The Anglicans were entering into a politically motivated agreement with the Prussians to have a bishop of Jerusalem who would exercise jurisdiction over Anglicans, Lutherans, and Calvinists alike. This scheme convinced Newman that the Church of England did not in fact cherish its Catholic heritage. He had to acknowledge that his theory of the *via media* had failed; that the Church of the *via media* existed only on paper. Such was the realization that shattered Newman's Anglo-Catholic allegiance.

Was there an alternative that would preserve his previous certitudes and set them in a broader context? The dilemma seemed to be that while the Roman Church had the better claim to Catholicity, it could not match the apostolicity of the Anglican communion. Thus neither Church could provide a home for Newman. As for Eastern Orthodoxy, Newman admired its patristic heritage but considered that it was too much linked to ethnicity and political governments to be a viable option for Anglicans in the nineteenth century.[27]

The seeds of a new approach were perhaps planted in Newman's mind by his Mediterranean trip of 1832–3. Although he was impressed by Greek Orthodox worship in Corfu, his imagination and heart were more deeply affected by his experiences in Italy and Sicily.

> [T]he sight of so many great places, venerable shrines, and noble churches, much impressed my imagination. And my heart was touched also. Making an expedition on foot across some wild country in Sicily, at six in the morning, I came upon a small church; I heard voices, and I looked in. It was crowded, and the congregation was singing. Of course it was the mass, though I did not know it at the time.[28]

He was also struck by the devoutness of the Roman seminarians, and by the maintenance of the rule of clerical celibacy, which he recognized as apostolic. Thus, even without participating in Roman Catholic worship, he learned to have tender feelings towards the Church of Rome, however faulty her doctrine might be. While waiting at Palermo he penned the verses:

> Oh that thy creed were sound!
> For thou dost soothe the heart, Thou Church of Rome,
>   By thy unwearied watch and varied round
> Of service, in thy Saviour's holy home.[29]

The favourable impression of Catholicism gained from his travels in Italy and Sicily helps to explain the way in which Newman would react, six years later, to Wiseman's article about the Donatists. The thought then came to him, for the first time: 'The Church of Rome will be found right after all.'[30] It was as if he had seen a ghost. He could never be again as if he had not seen it. A little later, while the controversy was swirling about Tract 90, he published a letter in which he seems to be alluding to the popular religion he had observed in Italy and Sicily:

> The age is moving towards something, and most unhappily the

one religious communion among us, which has of late years been practically in possession of this something, is the Church of Rome. She alone, amid all the errors and evils of her practical system, has given free scope to the feelings of awe, mystery, tenderness, reverence, devotedness, and other feelings which may especially be called Catholic.[31]

The presentiment that Rome might, after all, be right was not yet a solution to the crisis. In his perplexity Newman determined, as always, 'to be guided not by my imagination, but by my reason'.[32] Could he satisfy himself intellectually that the Roman Church, contrary to appearances, was apostolic? Could its additions to patristic teaching be viewed not as corruptions but as something else – namely true developments arising out of deeper insights into the apostolic faith? Newman's handling of these questions makes it clear that his ascending scale of belief contained safeguards against excesses of credulity.

Reflecting on Protestant objections to the Anglican acceptance of the early creeds and ecumenical councils, Newman had to recognize that there could be such a thing as legitimate development in doctrine. In order to judge whether the Roman doctrines as formulated, for example, at Trent were legitimate developments, Newman excogitated seven criteria, based on analogies from fields as various as biology and jurisprudence. In his *Essay on the Development of Christian Doctrine* he applied these criteria as tests to distinguish true developments in the Church from regressions or corruptions.

In this work of 1845, decisive for his final conversion, Newman directly addressed what had been his principal contention against Rome – namely that its distinctive doctrines and practices were external additions without any basis in revelation. If this were the case, acceptance of the Roman system would be an excess in the sphere of belief, a superstition.

Throughout the *Essay* this objection is never far from Newman's mind. He notes that classical Roman authors such as Pliny, Tacitus, and Suetonius, while they made different charges against the Christians, agreed on one point, that Christianity was a superstition. Celsus in his anti-Christian polemic accused the Christians of irrational credulity and of saying, in effect, 'Do not inquire, but believe.'[33] Thus the pagans of antiquity had rejected the Christian religion on almost the same grounds that Protestants and Anglicans were objecting to Roman Catholicism in Newman's own day.

In the course of his study Newman takes up, at different points, a whole series of Roman doctrines and practices that were allegedly superstitious – devotion to the Blessed Virgin and to the saints, veneration of relics, Purgatory, monastic vows, and the like. By calling attention to the presence of these same elements in early Christianity, he diverts the charge that they are Roman innovations. While conceding that in some cases these practices were taken over from paganism, he answers that what was superstitious in paganism need not be so in Christianity, since the Church has the power to sanctify these practices and direct them to the glory of God. Recalling a work he had reviewed for the *British Critic* in January 1841, he quotes Henry Hart Milman as arguing, 'These things are in heathenism, therefore they are not Christian.' Reversing the dictum, Newman prefers to say, 'These things are in Christianity, therefore they are not heathen.'[34] The Protestants, he remarks, are forever hunting for a fabulous primitive simplicity; he himself chooses to repose in Catholic fullness.[35]

The crux of Newman's argument is that corruptions, if they take hold of the Church as an institution, bring about weakness and decay. In Roman Catholicism he finds, on the contrary, a wonderful vigour and energy. Although it goes through periods of exhaustion and repose, it rises again, refreshed and restored. It undergoes changes, but they are not alien to its nature; rather they are consolidations and adaptations of what it has always been.[36]

Newman does not deny that members of the Catholic Church tend to fall into superstitions. This fault also occurred in the Church of the patristic Golden Age. John Chrysostom vehemently denounced the use of amulets by Christians and Augustine protested against abuses in the agapae.[37] The very abundance of sanctifying power in the Church, Newman observes, may constitute a standing temptation for people to seek to wrest that power to their own ends.[38] Later, writing as a Catholic, Newman would wonder 'whether that nation really had the faith, which is free in all its ranks and classes from all kinds and degrees of what is commonly called superstition'.[39] Wherever faith is 'vivid and earnest', Newman surmised, it will surely have superstition as its companion.[40] The holier the institution, the greater will be the likelihood of its debasement. *Corruptio optimi pessima.*

Newman did not propose his theory of the development of Christian doctrine as a demonstration that would prove the validity of Catholic Christianity to all and sundry. The theory was, as he himself declared, a hypothesis to answer a difficulty. It had the plausibility that one can expect from a good theory. It removed an intellectual obstacle to his own conversion and, in combination with other factors, enabled him to see the credibility of the claims made on behalf of the Catholic Church.

Beyond this conclusion a further step was necessary – that of actual submission. Like Charles Reding, the chief character of Newman's novel *Loss and Gain*, Newman felt the need of an oracle that would demand his faith. 'If no one claims my faith', asked Reding, 'how can I exercise it?'[41] To make an act of faith it was necessary to go out of oneself, to accept a standard above one's own reason. The decisive point was that the Catholic Church did claim to utter God's word with infallible assurance, and that in this claim it had no competitor. Having completed his personal investigation, Newman joyfully submitted to the authority of the Catholic Church, requesting 'admission into the one Fold of Christ'.[42]

Conclusion

Newman's three conversions all occurred more than a century ago and in a religious context rather different from our own. Besides, he was an exceptional person, endowed with vast intelligence and erudition. Few of us can approach, even remotely, his intuitive capacities and dialectical skills. For all these reasons Newman is a giant more easily admired than imitated.

Notwithstanding its uniqueness, however, Newman's religious pilgrimage has structural features in common with the stories of many other converts from Augustine to the present day. With his extraordinary gift of introspection, he makes it easier to identify some of these features.[43]

In the first place, Newman brings out the importance of a heart and an imagination attuned to the gospel message. Without a keen sensitivity to the voice of conscience and a devout aspiration to the fullness of religious truth, spiritual progress can scarcely be expected. The heart and the imagination supply the antecedent probability that normally enters into the process of discernment.

Closely connected with this first feature is a second: the value of concrete experiences and personal example to lead one forward in the quest for truth. Although study and abstract reasoning play a role in the process, they rarely, if ever, take the place of providential encounters such as those mentioned by Newman in his autobiography.

A third lesson that may be derived from Newman's story is the positive role that challenges can play in purifying and maturing one's faith. The very incapacity of a religious position to withstand objections may be seen as a providential opportunity to weed out some error or supply some element that is still lacking. Each of Newman's three conversions was provoked by challenges to his previous religious stance.

In the fourth place, Newman's journey of faith illustrates the need for caution in avoiding hasty and ill-considered decisions. He was scrupulously careful in seeking criteria to discriminate between authentic faith and superstition, and allowed sufficient time for his perceptions to mature. In that respect he differs from some who hastily converted and then relapsed, not having found what they imagined they would.

Finally, Newman can teach us the necessity of passing beyond private judgement and of submitting one's will and intellect to a divinely accredited organ or oracle of religious truth. There is a world of difference between those who adhere to a truth because they have personally reasoned it out and those who do so because it is contained in the word of God. As Newman clearly saw, only the second group may be said to have faith, in the theological sense of the term.

In the end, therefore, Newman's conversions, notwithstanding their highly individual character, do present a pattern for others. Precisely because of his eminence as a thinker and scholar, and his almost unequalled ability to articulate the probings of the religious heart, Newman is a master from whom much can be learned. His own struggles taught him a method of inquiry and discernment that can, to some extent, be used by all sincere religious seekers. The 150th anniversary of his conversion to the Catholic Church should offer an occasion for many of our own contemporaries to put themselves in the school of so great a master.

Notes

1. John Henry Newman, *Apologia pro vita sua*, ed. Ian Ker (London: Penguin, 1994), p. 182.
2. See John Henry Newman, *An Essay in Aid of a Grammar of Assent*, ed. Ian Ker (Oxford: Clarendon, 1985), note II, pp. 318–22.

3. *Tracts for the Times*, No. 85; reprinted in John Henry Newman, *Discussions and Arguments on Various Subjects of the Day* (London: Longmans, Green, and Co., 1899), Part III, pp. 109–253, at p. 200. Quoted in *An Essay on the Development of Christian Doctrine*, chap. V, sec. 6, §2 (Garden City, N.Y.: Doubleday Image, 1960), p. 202.

4. Journal entry of June or July 1821 in John Henry Newman, *Autobiographical Writings*, ed. Henry Tristram (London and New York: Sheed & Ward, 1956), p. 166.

5. Journal entry of 26 July 1826, *ibid.*, p. 172.

6. *Grammar of Assent*, chap. VII, §2, pp. 144–68.

7. John Henry Newman, *Loss and Gain: The Story of a Convert* (London: Longmans, Green, and Co., 1906), p. 333.

8. John Henry Newman, 'The Tamworth Reading Room', *Discussions and Arguments*, Part IV, pp. 254–305; quoted in *Grammar of Assent*, chap. IV, §1, pp. 65–6.

9. John Henry Newman, *Parochial and Plain Sermons* (San Francisco: Ignatius, 1987), VIII: 15, p. 1682.

10. *Apologia*, pp. 158–9.

11. John Henry Newman, *Discourses to Mixed Congregations* (London: Longmans, Green, and Co., 1897), Discourse X, 'Faith and Private Judgment', pp. 191–213.

12. *Grammar of Assent*, chap. VII, §2, p. 248.

13. *Apologia*, pp. 23–4.

14. *Grammar of Assent*, chap. IV, §2, pp. 77–8.

15. *Ibid.*, chap. IV, §1, pp. 42–4, at 43.

16. *Apologia*, p. 23.

17. *Ibid.*, p. 25.

18. Journal entry of 19 January 1823, *Autobiographical Writings*, p. 169.

19. John Henry Newman, 'On the Immortality of the Soul', *Parochial and Plain Sermons*, I: 2, p. 16.

20. *Apologia*, p. 26.

21. *Ibid.*

22. *Ibid.*, pp. 25–6.

23. 'Autobiographical Memoir III', *Autobiographical Writings*, p. 83.

24. *Apologia*, p. 33.

25. *Ibid.*, p. 37.

26. *Ibid.*, pp. 115–16.

27. For a more complete exposition of Newman's attitude toward Orthodoxy see Ian Ker, *Newman and the Fullness of Christianity* (Edinburgh: T. & T. Clark, 1993), chap. 5, 'Eastern Christianity', pp. 83–102.

28. *Apologia*, p. 65.

29. *Verses on Various Occasions* (London: Longmans, Green, and Co., 1983), p. 153. For a more complete presentation of Newman's impressions of Italian Catholicism than one finds in the *Apologia*, it is helpful to read his letters written at the time, published in *The Letters and Diaries of John Henry Newman*, 3 (Oxford: Clarendon, 1979). For discussion see Ian Ker, 'Newman's Conversion to the Catholic Church: Another Perspective', *Renascence* 43 (1990–91): 17–27.

30. *Apologia*, p. 116.

31. *Ibid.*, p. 157.

32. *Ibid.*, p. 117.

33. *Essay on Development*, chap. VI, sec. 1, §17, p. 227.

34. *Ibid.*, chap. VIII, §2, p. 359.

35. *Ibid.*, p. 360.

36. *Ibid.*, chap. XII, §9, p. 417.

37. *Ibid.*, chap. VIII, §2, no. 10, pp. 356–7.

38. *Ibid.*, p. 357.

39. John Henry Newman, Preface to the third edition (1877) of *The Via Media of the Anglican Church* (London: Longmans, Green and Co., 1901), vol. 1, p. lxix.

40. *Ibid.*, p. lxviii.

41. *Loss and Gain*, p. 227.

42. *Apologia*, p. 314.
43. Emilie Griffin in her work *Turning: Reflections on the Experience of Conversion* (Garden City, N.Y.: Doubleday, 1980), concludes that there are four stages in the typical conversion: 'First, there is Desire or longing; second, the Dialectic, or argumentative, reasoning phase; third, the Struggle or crisis; and finally, the Surrender' (p. 29). It would not be difficult to identify all these stages in each of Newman's conversions.

3

Newman's Post-Conversion Discovery of Catholicism

Ian Ker

I

The story of John Henry Newman's conversion to Catholicism is not quite the same as the story of his discovery of Catholicism. The *Apologia pro vita sua*, which is subtitled 'Being a History of his Religious Opinions', is in effect his theological autobiography up to the year 1845 when he joined the Roman Catholic Church. In it we find a detailed account of the development of his ideas but barely anything of his inner spiritual life or of his wider religious experience. The aim of the book is to show how one man was led on logically and naturally from a belief in Christianity to belief in Catholicism. It was important for Newman to demonstrate not only the sincerity of his conversion but also its intellectual objectivity. As a result, other elements and factors are rigorously excluded, thus giving an impression of an austerely cerebral approach to religion, which was far from true of the man.

Nevertheless, it is the case that Newman's intellectual conversion did for the most part precede a more experiential and imaginative discovery of Catholicism. He became a Catholic, he always used to say afterwards, because he became convinced that 'the modern Roman Communion was the heir and the image of the primitive Church'.[1] Now while Newman knew a very great deal about the early Church, he knew extraordinarily little about contemporary Catholicism, apart from its formal doctrines and teaching. In 1835, two years after the beginning of the Oxford Movement, he had admitted to wanting 'to fall across a Romanist to get into their system', but he was averse to 'getting intimate'

with any English Catholics because of their hostility to the
Church of England and their readiness to enter into alliance with
its political enemies.[2] However, what is interesting is that he saw
quite clearly that one could not understand Catholicism merely
by reading books about it, as there was no substitute for actually
getting to know real Catholics so as to learn about the Catholic
Church from within. In 1844, when he had all but decided to become a Roman Catholic, he could even say: 'I have no existing
sympathies with Roman Catholics. I hardly ever, even abroad,
was at one of their services – I know nothing of them. I do not
like what I hear of them.'[3]

This is something of an exaggeration, since, as Newman gladly
acknowledged in the *Apologia*, there was a Roman Catholic who
had significantly influenced his conversion – a young Irish priest
called Charles Russell, a professor at Maynooth, who had taken
the initiative in writing to Newman and sending him a volume of
St Alfonso Liguori's sermons, in the hope that practical writings
of this kind would do far more to make Catholicism better
known and more attractive to English people than theology or
apologetics. Russell could hardly have chosen more daringly, as
the Neapolitan saint was a favourite target for anti-Catholic
polemic because of his allegedly notorious Mariolatry. In reality,
Newman found nothing of the kind, and the fact that certain
passages had been admittedly omitted from one sermon on the
Virgin Mary seemed to him to show that Catholic spirituality
varied from country to country and was not as uniform as he had
supposed. Russell had actually called on Newman a couple of
times in Oxford, and 'he had, perhaps, more to do with my conversion than any one else'.[4]

Still, it was true that Newman had avoided Catholics and
Catholic churches – except, that is, when he was on his
Mediterranean tour of 1832–3, and when he could hardly help
being exposed to both. Even then, he had 'religiously abstained
from acts of worship, though it was a most soothing comfort' to
go into churches, where, however, he claimed not to 'know what
was going on; I neither understood nor tried to understand the
Mass service'.[5] Like the relevant part of the *Apologia*, this passage
from a post-conversion letter hardly does justice to the effect on
Newman of visiting Catholic countries and seeing Catholicism
for the first time at first hand.

Nevertheless, the *Apologia* does make some reference to the
emotional and imaginative influence on his development of actu-

ally experiencing for himself a religion which, since his early Evangelically-inspired conversion of 1816, he had regarded as the religion of the Antichrist predicted in the Bible. In the first chapter, where he gives a summary account of these momentous months in his life, when for the first time he travelled abroad and witnessed both Catholicism in Italy and Malta and Orthodoxy in the Greek islands, he claims that 'I saw nothing but what was external: of the hidden life of Catholics I knew nothing'. But in the second chapter he effectively modifies this by admitting that he was certainly affected, indeed impressed, not to say moved, by what he saw:

> [W]hen I was abroad, the sight of so many great places, venerable shrines, and noble churches, much impressed my imagination. And my heart was touched also. Making an expedition on foot across some wild country in Sicily, at six in the morning, I came upon a small church; I heard voices, and I looked in. It was crowded, and the congregation was singing. Of course it was the mass, though I did not know it at the time. And, in my weary days at Palermo, I was not ungrateful for the comfort which I had received in frequenting the churches; nor did I ever forget it. . . . Thus I learned to have tender feelings towards her [the Catholic Church]; but still my reason was not affected at all.[6]

If one looks at the many letters Newman wrote home during the six months and more that he was away, one cannot help but be struck by the schizophrenic attitude he finds himself adopting towards Catholicism. On the one hand, he retains all his theological objections to Tridentine Catholicism, objections which in some cases were only reinforced by the apparent scandals and superstitious practices he observed; on the other hand, not only is he clearly surprised by how much seemed quite unobjectionable and even admirable, but above all the effect of being in Rome itself was quite devastating. He thought it 'a wonderful place', 'of all cities the first', and all the cities he had ever seen were 'but as dust, even dear Oxford inclusive, compared with its majesty and glory'. But he was also affected by very different feelings. After all, Rome bore an 'awful' aspect as 'the great Enemy of God': its

> immense . . . ruins, the thought of the purposes to which they were dedicated, the sight of the very arena where Ignatius suffered, the columns of heathen pride with the inscriptions still legible – brand it as the vile tool of God's wrath and again Satan's malice.

Again and again in his letters to England, he spoke of his 'mingled feelings' about the city:

> You are in the place of martyrdom and burial of Apostles and Saints – you have about you the buildings and sights they saw – and you are in the city to which England owes the blessing of the gospel – But then on the other hand the superstitions; – or rather, what is far worse, the solemn reception of them as an essential part of Christianity – but then again the extreme beauty and costliness of the Churches – and then on the contrary the knowledge that the most famous was built (in part) by the scale of indulgences – Really this is a cruel place. – There is more and more to be seen and thought of, daily – it is a mine of all sorts of excellences, but the very highest.[7]

Captivated as he obviously was by Rome, he felt obliged nevertheless to continue to protest against its unreformed religion:

> I cannot quite divest myself of the notion that Rome Christian is somehow under an especial shade as Rome Pagan certainly was – though I have seen nothing here to confirm it. Not that one can tolerate for an instant the wretched perversion of the truth which is sanctioned here, but I do not see my way enough to say that there is anything peculiar in the condition of Rome. . . .[8]

True, it had to be admitted, there were 'great appearances . . . of piety in the Churches', but nonetheless as a 'system' Catholicism was undoubtedly 'corrupt'.[9] Thus, when he saw the Pope and his 'court' at high mass, he was scandalized by the 'unedifying dumbshow',

> yet as I looked on, and saw . . . the Holy Sacrament offered up, and the blessing given, and recollected I was in church, I could only say in very perplexity my own words, 'How shall I name thee, Light of the wide west, or heinous error-seat?' – and felt the force of the parable of the tares – who can separate the light from the darkness but the Creator Word who prophesied their union? And so I am forced to leave the matter, not at all seeing my way out of it. – How shall I name thee?[10]

He was to ponder that question for a long time. In the meantime, he contented himself with trying to distinguish between 'the Roman C. system' which he had 'ever detested' and 'the *Catholic* system' to which he confessed himself 'more attached than ever'. And while he feared that 'there are very grave and farspreading scandals among the Italian priesthood, and there is mummery in abundance', he could not help thinking that 'there is a deep substratum of true Christianity, and I think they may be as near truth (at the least) as that Mr. B. whom I like less and less every day'. Mr Burgess was the Church of England chaplain in Rome, whom Newman described as 'one of the most perfect watering place preachers I ever heard, most painfully so – pompous in manner and matter'.[11] The 'individual members of the cruel church', on the contrary, 'who can but love and feel for them?' The baffling paradox was that in these very followers of the Antichrist who condemned Protestants as heretics, Newman found 'so much amiableness and gentleness' and (the highest compliment) 'so much Oxonianism'.[12] At the time he did not realize the disturbing implications of the corruption he saw or thought he saw – 'the lamentable mixture of truth with error which Romanism exhibits – the corruption of the highest and noblest views and principles, far higher than we Protestants have, with malignant poisons'.[13] Much later, as a Catholic, he was to develop a veritable theology of corruption, but for the time being he did not appreciate the momentous corollary of the principle that the corruption of the best is the worst.

The only explanation he could provide at the time was that there was an important distinction between Rome as a place (according to Protestant mythology one of the four beasts of the Apocalypse) and as a church: but 'how a distinction is to be drawn between two powers, spiritual and devilish, which are so strongly united, is . . . beyond our imagination'. He could only attribute the corruption of Roman Catholicism to the fact that it was the 'slave' of the evil spirit which must still be ruling Rome.[14]

As he waited for a ship to take him back to England from Palermo after his nearly fatal illness in Sicily, he felt 'calmed' by visits to churches – although he still 'knew nothing of the Presence of the Blessed Sacrament there', nor did he attend any services.[15] But the 'still retreats' which the cool churches offered from 'the city's sultry streets' inspired the deeply ambivalent poem which begins

> Oh that thy creed were sound!
> For thou dost soothe the heart, Thou Church of Rome,
> By thy unwearied watch and varied round
> Of service, in thy Saviour's holy home.[16]

Twelve years were to pass before Newman was to become convinced that it was the Roman Catholic Church's creed that was 'sound' and that it was the Anglican position that was unsound.

During those years he was never again to come into the same kind
of close contact with Catholicism as he had experienced during
those exciting, traumatic months away from England. The
profound revolution in his theological views from Calvinist
Evangelicalism to Roman Catholicism was the result of a gradual
development that culminated in the recognition that the Church
of the Fathers was the same church as that modern church which
alone dared call itself simply 'the Catholic Church'. In his own
words, it was 'the living picture' that 'history presents' which
finally opened his eyes to an identity that he admitted was not
self-evident. And it was to that first 'vision of the Fathers' which
his boyhood reading of the Calvinist Joseph Milner's history of
the church had so vividly impressed on his mind, that he ultimately traced his conversion: 'The Fathers made me a Catholic.'[17]
However difficult it might be to show someone else the close resemblance that he saw between modern Catholicism and early
Christianity, nevertheless it did seem obvious to him in later years
that 'the present Roman Catholic Church is *the only Church*
which is like, and it is very like, the primitive Church' –

> It is almost like a photograph of the primitive Church; or at least
> it does not differ from the primitive Church near so much as the
> photograph of a man of 40 differs from his photograph when 20.
> *You know that it is the same man.*[18]

Even so, Newman was still remarkably ignorant at the time of
his conversion of the concrete system of Catholicism as it had developed through the middle ages and since the Council of Trent.
In fact, the feature of his new religious life that most struck him
came as a complete surprise to him.

> We went over not realizing those privileges which we have found
> *by* going. I never allowed my mind to dwell on what I might gain
> of blessedness – but certainly, if I had thought much upon it, I
> could not have fancied the extreme, ineffable comfort of being in
> the same house with Him who cured the sick and taught His dis-
> ciples ... When I have been in Churches abroad, I have religiously
> abstained from acts of worship, though it was a most soothing
> comfort to go into them – nor did I know what was going on; I
> neither understood nor tried to understand the Mass service – and
> I did not know, or did not observe, the tabernacle Lamp – but
> now after tasting of the awful delight of worshipping God in His
> Temple, how unspeakably cold is the idea of a Temple without
> that Divine Presence! One is tempted to say what is the meaning,
> what is the use of it?[19]

It is striking how it was the reservation of the sacrament in the tabernacle in Catholic churches that more than anything else impressed and moved Newman. This is not what we might expect a convert as ignorant about Catholic devotional life as Newman claims he was, to emphasize above everything else, including the mass and the ritual. And it tells us, I suggest, something very important not only about Newman but also about a central aspect of the impact of Catholicism on the imagination of the English Protestant convert. Thus, when Newman informs a close Anglican friend,

> I am writing next room to the Chapel – It is such an incomprehensible blessing to have Christ in bodily presence in one's house, within one's walls, as swallows up all other privileges ... To know that He is close by – to be able again and again through the day to go in to Him ...[20]

he is not only making a devotional or spiritual point. He is also saying something very significant about objectivity and reality. For it was this concrete presence in a material tabernacle which above all for Newman at any rate produced 'the deep impression of religion as an objective fact' that so struck him about Catholicism – far more, for instance, than its discipline or its fervour. He admired in those early days 'every where the signs of an awful and real system'. Moreover, objectivity and reality also meant practicality: instead of being 'a vague generality' or merely 'an idea', Catholicism as compared with Anglicanism struck him as 'a working religion'. Had he not previously, he acknowledged, 'kept aloof from Catholics from a sense of duty' but 'known them and their religion from personal acquaintance', he would have been 'exposed to a set of influences in their favour, from which in matter of fact' he 'was debarred'.[21] In Newman's case, in other words, the discovery of Catholicism was a consequence rather than a cause of conversion.

When Newman arrived in Italy nearly a year after his becoming a Catholic, he was immediately and vividly aware of a reality that powerfully impinged on his consciousness, but of which he had been quite oblivious on his previous visit. Arriving in Milan, he immediately noticed that he had now an added reason for preferring classical to gothic architecture, since its simplicity meant that the high altar stood out as the focal point of the church, which meant that the reserved sacrament had particular prominence – for 'Nothing moves there but the distant glimmering

Lamp which betokens the Presence of our Undying Life, hidden but ever working'. His almost obsessive preoccupation with this 'Real Presence' goes further than the devotional: 'It is really most wonderful to see this Divine Presence looking out almost into the open streets from the various Churches. ... I never knew what worship was, as an objective fact, till I entered the Catholic Church.'[22] For what Newman had discovered was that the objectivity of the worship which so impressed him – and nothing else about the worship attracted his attention in the same way – only reflected the objectivity of Catholicism, which he came to believe was a quite different kind of religion from Anglicanism or Protestantism. Now he was delighted to find, as he thought, 'a real religion – not a mere opinion such, that you have no confidence that your next door neighbour holds it too, but an external objective substantive creed and worship'.[23]

Again, linked to this was the discovery of a highly practical kind of religion: instead of being something very special and removed from the ordinary mundane world, Catholicism, for all its supernatural claims – and, ever since that Mediterranean tour, it had always seemed to Newman a much more spiritual religion than that of the Church of England – seemed also, paradoxically, a far more matter-of-fact kind of 'business':

> a Catholic Cathedral is a sort of world, every one going about his own business, but that business a religious one; groups of worshippers, and solitary ones – kneeling, standing – some at shrines, some at altars – hearing Mass and communicating – currents of worshippers intercepting and passing by each other – altar after altar lit up for worship, like stars in the firmament – or the bell giving notice of what is going on in parts you do not see – and all the while the canons in the choir going through matins and lauds, and at the end of it the incense rolling up from the high altar ... lastly, all of this without any show or effort, but what everyone is used to – every one at his own work, and leaving every one else to his.[24]

Newman's fascination with the reservation of the sacrament also reflects his celebrated philosophical distinction between the notional and the real: whereas notions are intellectual abstractions, reality is what we personally experience in the appropriate concrete form. Dogmatic as Catholicism is, it is not, Newman insisted, exactly a religion of dogmas, for what Catholics worship, he claimed, are not theological definitions but 'Christ Himself, as He is represented in concrete existence in the Gospels'. It is, then, to assist and enable this worship of the person of Christ that the consecrated bread is reserved in a prominent place in Catholic churches: 'Do we not believe in a Presence in the sacred Tabernacle, not as a form of words, or as a notion, but as an Object as real as we are real?'[25]

An important part of Newman's apologetic for Catholicism lies in trying to show how different a religion in kind it is from Protestantism – that it is not as if Protestantism, seen from the Catholic perspective, is simply a truncated form of Catholicism, or Catholicism, from the Protestant point of view, is essentially Protestantism plus a whole lot of more or less undesirable accretions or corruptions. To one inquirer he wrote, 'I do not disguise that Catholicism is a *different religion* from Anglicanism.' To the convert, he explained, Christianity is no longer something that you merely experience privately in your own heart or construct in your own mind from reading the Bible; it is now a reality that exists independently of the subjective self and that envelopes one, so

> that the Atonement of Christ is not a thing at a distance, or like the sun standing over against us and separated off from us, but . . . we are surrounded by an *atmosphere* and are in a medium, through which his warmth and light flow in upon us on every side. . . .[26]

This reality of Christ, for Newman, is experienced not only through the reservation of the sacrament, but also through the whole Catholic system of sacraments and sacramentals, as well as the crucifixes and statues and pictures that surround the worshipper in a Catholic church. And the ultimate authority for one's religious beliefs is no longer oneself but the Church: 'consider the vast difference between believing in a living authority, unerring because divine, in matters of doctrine, and believing none; – between believing what an external authority defines, and believing what we ourselves happen to define as contained in Scripture'. This was why Newman was never in the least sanguine about reunion between the Church of England and the Church of Rome:

> it is a mere deceit, I fully think, to suppose that the difference between Catholics and Anglicans is, that one believes a little more, and the other a little less; and therefore that they could unite. The religions never could unite . . . because they proceed on different *ideas*; and, if they look in certain external aspects alike, or have doctrines in common, yet the way in which those doctrines are held, and the whole internal structure in the two religions is dif-

ferent; so that, even what a person has before he is a Catholic, being grafted on a new stock, becomes new, and he is like a Jew become Christian.[27]

Whatever the element of exaggeration in this stark analysis, Newman never substantially changed his mind in later years.

II

This whole post-conversion process of discovering Catholicism was not only of theological significance, for, as we have already seen from his letters, it also powerfully engaged Newman's imagination. Certainly, it provided much of the creative stimulus that produced the most overtly literary period in his life, when he deliberately abstained from theology and instead turned to writing Catholic apologetics in the form of novels and satire. The book that he himself always considered his 'best written book',[28] although sadly it must be one of his least read works, was *Lectures on the Present Position of Catholics in England*, published in 1851. It contains some of the finest prose satire in the language, Swiftian in its savage imagery and grotesque in the vein of Dickens, whose satiric portrait of Mr Podsnap in *Our Mutual Friend* (1865) is remarkably anticipated in one glorious passage on John Bull's chauvinism.[29] The delivery of these lectures was a significant moment in English cultural history, as for the first time since the Reformation a writer of genius confronted head-on the triumphalism of the 'no Popery' tradition, which had captured the popular imagination.

There is a passage in *Present Position of Catholics* which is worth quoting at some length because, for Newman, it evokes the utterly alien atmosphere of a Catholic church as it may strike a Protestant observer.

> One day he pays a visit to some Catholic chapel, or he casually finds the door open, and walks in. He enters and gazes about him, with a mixed feeling of wonder, expectation and disgust; and according to circumstances, this or that feeling predominates, and shows itself in his bearing and his countenance. In one man it is curiosity; in another, scorn; in another, conscious superiority; in another, abhorrence; over all their faces, however, there is a sort of uncomfortable feeling, as if they were in the cave of Trophonius or in a Mesmerist's lecture-room. One and all seem to believe that something strange and dreadful may happen any moment; and they crowd up together, as if some great ceremony is going on,

tiptoeing and staring, and making strange faces, like the gargoyles or screen ornaments of the church itself. Every sound of the bell, every movement of the candles, every change in the grouping of the sacred ministers and the assistants, puts their hands and limbs in motion, to see what is coming next; our own poor alleviation, in thinking of them, lying in this, – that they are really ignorant of what is going on, and miss, even with their bodily eyes, the distinctive parts of the rite. What is our ground of comfort, however, will be their ground of accusation against us; for they are sure to go away and report that our worship consists of crossings, bowing, genuflections, incensings, locomotions, and revolvings, all about nothing.[30]

Part of the Protestant's incomprehension lies simply in his ignorance of what is going on; but there is, Newman thought, a deeper reason for his bewilderment, which concerns the very nature of the worship rather than its exact meaning. For Newman's point is that there is a real sense in which comprehension is impossible, since Catholic worship, which is essentially dramatic as it consists in liturgical action, is incommensurate with Protestant worship which is a religion of the word. In Protestant churches words are read and said and sung, accompanied by the minimum of action; in Catholic churches it is the words which accompany the liturgical and sacramental actions. Far from Catholic worship consisting in mere actions signifying nothing beyond themselves, Newman was now in effect struck by the force of the saying that actions speak louder than words.

As an Anglican, Newman had written 'Life is for action.'[31] But 'life', he had also insisted, was a note of the Church; and as a Tractarian he had been preoccupied with trying to show that the Church of England contained a 'living principle', a note of the Church 'equal to any',[32] a view that seemed to be supported by the extraordinary 'burst of hidden life' that the Oxford Movement had aroused and which seemed to him 'the greatest note of the Catholicity of our Church'.[33] A church, therefore, that was living would be characterized by a life of action. On the eve of the Movement he had contrasted 'that fresh vigorous Power of . . . the first centuries' and 'the joyous swing of her advance' with the 'do-nothing perplexity' of the Church of England.[34] Action meant life, and it was action that Newman found in Catholicism, not least in its worship. It was no longer a matter simply of saying words; things happened. The undergraduate hero of *Loss and Gain* wonders, 'Why can only a clergyman read prayers in church? – Why cannot I?'[35] There is no answer to that question, he discovers, unless the clergyman is seen as a priest who alone can perform certain sacramental actions, as in 'that Church which really breathes and lives'.[36]

In *Difficulties Felt by Anglicans*, the set of lectures which preceded *Present Position of Catholics* in 1850, and which were intended to persuade Anglo-Catholics to follow him into the Roman Catholic Church, Newman describes the difference between the faith of Protestants and that of Catholics by arguing that the former hold religious opinions, while for the latter the objects of belief are simply facts:

> Just as in England, the whole community, whatever the moral state of the individuals, *knows* about railroads and electric telegraphs; and about the Court, and men in power, and proceedings in Parliament; and about religious controversies, and about foreign affairs, and about all that is going on around and beyond them: so, in a Catholic country, the ideas of heaven and hell, Christ and the evil spirit, saints, angels, souls in purgatory, grace, the Blessed Sacrament, the sacrifice of the Mass, absolution, indulgences, the virtue of relics, of holy images, of holy water, and of other holy things, are of the nature of *facts*, which all men, good and bad, young and old, rich and poor, take for granted. They are facts brought home to them by faith. . . .

To prove his point, Newman avers that if you were to 'Set up a large Crucifix at Charing Cross; the police would think you simply insane.'[37]

But a faith which sees things or facts is also, according to Newman, a faith that may not be accompanied by the appropriate moral state, as he graphically illustrates with a vivid scene, again exemplifying the kind of activity and movement in Catholic churches that had made such a deep impression on him.

> You enter into one of the churches close upon the scene of festivity, and you turn our eyes towards a confessional. The penitents are crowding for admission, and they seem to have no shame, or solemnity, or reserve about the errand on which they are come; till at length, on a penitent's turning from the grate, one tall woman, bolder than a score of men, darts forward from a distance into the place he has vacated, to the disappointment of the many who have waited longer than she. You almost groan under the weight of your imagination that such a soul, so selfish, so unrecollected, must surely be in very ill dispositions for so awful a sacrament. You look at the priest, and he has on his face a look almost of im-

patience, or of good-natured compassion, at the voluble and superfluous matter which is the staple of her confession. The priests, you think, are no better than the people....

There is a feeble old woman, who first genuflects before the Blessed Sacrament, and then steals her neighbour's handkerchief, or prayer-book, who is intent on her devotions. ... She worships and she sins; she kneels because she believes, she steals because she does not love....

Newman goes on to describe the fiesta scene outside the church, so calculated to shock Protestant susceptibilities. It is not only the popular superstition and corruption –

You come out again and mix in the idle and dissipated throng, and you fall in with a man in a palmer's dress, selling false relics, and a credulous circle of customers buying them as greedily as though they were the supposed French laces and India silks of a pedlar's basket

– but the extraordinary mingling of the religious and the secular. The town's guilds are laying on a play about the creation – but

the *chef d'oeuvre* of the exhibition is the display of fireworks to be let off as the *finale*. 'How unutterably profane!' again you cry. Yes, profane to you ... profane to a population which only half believes; not profane to those who, however coarse-minded, however sinful, believe wholly ... They gaze, and, in drinking in the exhibition with their eyes, they are making one continuous and intense act of faith.[38]

This intensity, however, in Newman's eyes, bore no relation to the seriousness of Protestantism, which, in 'reforming' Catholicism, had fenced off religion from the rest of ordinary life, and turned it into something special and removed from day-to-day living. The relief of finding religion integrated again into life more than compensated in his view for the kind of corruption that he thought was inseparable from a living religion: 'Things that do not admit of abuse have very little life in them.'[39]

As an Anglican, Newman had felt that Catholic priests did not have the 'pompousness' of the clergy of the established Church.[40] It had not apparently occurred to him then that a popular religion, which was notoriously characterized by superstition and vulgarity, was hardly likely to possess the kind of pomposity that seemed to belong to Anglicanism, which, unlike Methodism, for instance, has never really been a 'popular' religion, except in the ritualistic Anglo-Catholicism that, in a later phase of

Tractarianism, established itself in the slums of the industrial cities. In a private memorandum he wrote as a Catholic, Newman observed that the Protestantism of the Church of England (he expressly excepted the embellishments of Anglo-Catholicism) could hardly be '*less* adapted to popularity ... it goes as near to the wind, as a religion can'. Apart from the unappealing sabbatarianism favoured by Evangelicals, he had even as an Anglican himself 'shivered' at the 'dreary' liturgy of the Book of Common Prayer (he was, of course, speaking of its devotional rather than literary qualities).[41]

Dignity and good taste were not qualities one necessarily found in Catholicism, but what Newman did think he had found was *life*, whether it was the popular devotions in the churches or the hidden contemplation of the enclosed cloister. In both cases, the worshipper seemed to be actively directed to an external, objective reality, as Newman attempts to show in the passage that ends his account of this imaginary Catholic mise-en-scène:

> You turn to go home, and, on your way, you pass through a retired quarter of the city. Look up at those sacred windows ... Seclusion, silence, watching, meditation, is their life day and night. The immaculate Lamb of God is ever before the eyes of the worshippers; or at least the invisible mysteries of faith ever stand out, as if in bodily shape, before their mental gaze.[42]

There is a further point that Newman draws out in his concluding reflections. For if 'faith impresses the mind with supernatural truths, as if it were sight', then 'the faith of this man, and the faith of that, is one and the same, and creates one and the same impression'. This meant that religion was not a private, subjective affair of an introverted nature, Newman claimed:

> It is just the reverse among a Protestant people; private judgment does but create opinions, and nothing more; and these opinions are peculiar to each individual, and different from those of any one else. Hence it leads men to keep their feelings to themselves, because the avowal of them only causes in others irritation or ridicule.

We shall be returning to this idea of Catholicism as liberating one from the prison of self; but in the meantime it is worth noting the interesting link Newman makes between the inherently uncertain nature of a religion, for which one is oneself the ultimate authority, and the quality of pomposity:

Since, too, they have no certainty of the doctrines they profess, they do but feel that they *ought* to believe them, and they try to believe them, and they nurse the offspring of their reason, as a sickly child, bringing it out of doors only on fine days. They feel quite clear and quite satisfied, while they are very still; but if they turn about their head, or change their posture ever so little, the vision of the Unseen, like a mirage, is gone from them. So they keep the exhibition of their faith for high days and great occasions, when it comes forth with sufficient pomp and gravity of language, and ceremonial of manner. Truths slowly totter out with Scripture texts at their elbow, as unable to walk alone. Moreover, Protestants know, if such and such things *be* true, what *ought* to be the voice, the tone, the gesture, and the carriage attendant upon them; thus reason, which is the substance of their faith, supplies also the rubrics, as I may call them, of their behaviour. This some . . . call reverence; though I am obliged to say it is . . . a mannerism, and an unpleasant mannerism . . . They condemn Catholics, because, however religious they may be, they are natural, unaffected, easy, and cheerful, in their mention of sacred things; and they think themselves never so real as when they are especially solemn.[43]

Newman was thinking specifically of the 'parsonic voice' Anglican clergy are famous for using in church, a voice which may seem not only to seal off religion in a special compartment from ordinary life, but also to introduce the important element of class, since the 'parsonic voice' carries distinct social overtones. Certainly, in the nineteenth century the Anglican clergyman was above all a 'gentleman', distinguished by class and education from the majority of his congregation.

In Newman's first novel, *Loss and Gain: The Story of a Convert*, published in 1848, the hero visits a Catholic church for the first time and exclaims to himself, 'This *is* a popular religion.' Having always been given to understand that Catholic worship was essentially 'formal and external' – after all, Catholicism was notoriously priest-ridden with its clerical ritual and Latin liturgy – Charles Reding is astonished to discover that 'it seems to possess all classes . . . indiscriminately'. One might have thought that the vernacular language of the Prayer Book would make the liturgy of the Church of England much more accessible to the people, but, although 'The words were Latin . . . every one seemed to understand them thoroughly'.

Reding thought he never had been present at worship before, so absorbed was the attention, so intense was the devotion of the congregation. What particularly struck him was, that whereas in the Church of England the clergyman or the organ was everything and the people nothing, except so far as the clerk is their representative, here it was just reversed. The priest hardly spoke, or at least audibly; but the whole congregation was as though one vast instrument or Panharmonicum, moving all together, and what was most remarkable, as if self-moved. They did not seem to require any one to prompt or direct them, though in the Litany the choir took the alternate parts.[44]

After Newman became a Catholic, he commented not only on the 'simple, natural, unaffected faith' of the Catholic clergy,[45] but also on the fact that they were not required to be educated in the sense of receiving a liberal education at the university, but rather that they had to undergo professional training in the seminary for the priesthood, which in a sense was a profession like any other.[46] Very different was the typical Church of England clergyman who had received a classical education but usually only the most rudimentary theological formation, at least until the foundation of Anglican theological colleges in the latter half of the nineteenth century. Unlike the Catholic priest with his clearly defined sacramental function and the Dissenting minister with his preaching ministry, the Anglican clergyman seemed less of a professional and more of an amateur – and therefore a gentleman. His most characteristic clerical task was reading the services in the Prayer Book. But it was not all clear why he and he only could do this. When Charles Reding raises the question, he is directed by another character in the novel to Jeremy Bentham's sarcastic proposal that

> a parish-boy should be taught to read the Liturgy ... Why send a person to the University for three or four years at an enormous expense, why teach him Latin and Greek, on purpose to read what any boy could be taught to read at a dame's school? What is the *virtue* of a clergyman's reading?[47]

Dickens makes exactly the same point in *Great Expectations* in his comic sketch of Mr Wopsle, the parish church clerk, who

> had a deep voice which he was uncommonly proud of; indeed it was understood among his acquaintance that if you could only give him his head, he would read the clergyman into fits; he himself confessed that if the Church was 'thrown open', meaning to competition, he would not despair of making his mark in it. The Church not being 'thrown open', he was, as I have said, our clerk.

But he punished the Amens tremendously; and when he gave out the psalm – always giving the whole verse – he looked all round the congregation first, as much as to say, 'You have heard our friend overhead; oblige me with your opinion of this style!'[48]

So far as Mr Wopsle is concerned, the professional expertise of the clergyman consists in his reading the service, which he, Mr Wopsle, can do at least as well. What the clerk, of course, lacks is not professional training but the birth and education which would make him a gentleman. And the fact the he is not an educated gentleman means, of course, that he cannot read the sonorous cadences of the Prayer Book in the same way that his vicar can. The point is too obvious to Dickens and his readers to need comment or explanation.

Reading and appreciating the beautiful prose of the Prayer Book requires education and taste. But as Willis, the Catholic convert in *Loss and Gain*, remarks, 'The idea of worship is different in the Catholic Church from the idea of it in your Church; for, in truth, the *religions* are different.' Catholic worship does not essentially consist in reading out words:

'I could attend Masses for ever and not be tired. It is not a mere form of words, – it is a great action, the greatest action that can be on earth. It is, not the invocation merely, but, if I dare use the word, the evocation of the Eternal. He becomes present on the altar in flesh and blood, before whom angels bow and devils tremble.'

A verbal, cerebral religion requires education and intelligence; the Catholic mass, by contrast, is a drama centred on an event that is equally accessible to all the worshippers:

'Each in his place, with his own heart, with his own wants, with his own thoughts, with his own intention, with his own prayers, separate but concordant, watching what is going on, watching its progress, uniting in its consummation; – not painfully and hopelessly following a hard form of prayer from beginning to end, but, like a concert of musical instruments, each different, but concurring in a sweet harmony. . . .'[49]

Allowing for the element of convert enthusiasm on Newman's part, there is an important point being made here about the essentially egalitarian nature of a liturgy which depends on a sacramental action rather than 'a hard form of prayer' requiring concentration 'from beginning to end', a clear reference, of course, to the measured, solemn prose of the Prayer Book.

At the end of the novel it is not the mass that Reding witnesses but the service of benediction:

> A cloud of incense was rising on high; the people suddenly all bowed low; what could it mean? the truth flashed on him, fearfully yet sweetly; it was the Blessed Sacrament – it was the Lord Incarnate who was on the altar, who had come to visit and to bless His people. It was the Great Presence, which makes a Catholic Church different from every other place in the world....[50]

The next and final chapter again finds the newly converted Charles Reding praying in front of the reserved sacrament after his reception into the Catholic Church. And so the novel ends on this strongly autobiographical theme of the objective reality of Catholicism.

Now there is no doubt that Newman was reacting against more than what he would have seen as the inevitable subjectivism of Anglicanism or Protestantism. It was his adolescent Evangelicalism which followed his conversion experience in 1816 that had left a lasting horror in him of religious introspection. The Evangelical insistence on justification by faith alone as being at the heart of Christianity meant, Newman came passionately to feel, that religion was turned into a matter of feelings: 'Instead of looking off to Jesus, and thinking little of ourselves, it is ... thought necessary ... to examine the heart with a view of ascertaining whether it is in a spiritual state or not.' The 'inherent mischief' of the doctrine, Newman explained, lay 'in its necessarily involving a continual self-contemplation and reference to self':

> He who aims at attaining sound doctrine or right practice, more or less looks out of himself; whereas, in labouring after a certain frame of mind, there is an habitual reflex action of the mind upon itself ... for, as if it were not enough for a man to look up simply to Christ for salvation, it is declared to be necessary that he should be able to recognise this in himself....[51]

The consequence, then, of this theology of justification seemed to Newman to be psychological and spiritual introspection:

> a system of doctrine has risen up during the last three centuries, in which faith or spiritual-mindedness is contemplated and rested on as the end of religion instead of Christ ... And in this way religion is made to consist in contemplating ourselves instead of Christ; not simply in looking to Christ, but in ascertaining that we look to Christ, not in His Divinity and Atonement, but in our conversion and our faith in those truths.[52]

The extent to which this acute sense of self-imprisonment affected Newman can be gauged by his description of the heroine's conversion in his second novel, *Callista* (1856). The story is set in the third century, and so it is, Newman is well aware, a very different kind of Catholic Christianity from the Tridentinism of the nineteenth century. But while any portrayal of the tabernacle with the reserved sacrament on the altar in the early Church would have been a complete anachronism, the external objective reality of Christianity is very much to the fore of the novel. This is shown nowhere more strikingly than in the most fundamental consideration that draws the pagan Callista to the Christian faith. Given that Newman is particularly associated with the argument from conscience as the best philosophical ground for theism, it is certainly remarkable how little part it plays in the only actual dramatization of this conversion process that he ever wrote. For what proves to be decisive is Callista's objection to the Christian doctrine of Hell which the priest Caecilius turns on its head by explaining that Hell is nothing other than the eternal prison of the self cut off from God. If there is any life after death, then

'you will still live . . . you will still be *you*. You will still be the same being, but deprived of those outward stays and reliefs and solaces, which, such as they are, you now enjoy. You will be yourself, shut up in yourself. I have heard that people go mad at length when placed in solitary confinement.'

Similarly, when Juba finds himself possessed by an evil spirit, he hears it cry, 'You cannot escape from yourself!' The happiness of the self depends on there being a reality outside of itself, for 'the soul always needs external objects to rest upon'. If, then, ordinary human affectivity demands the existence of other people, so too human beings have religious 'needs, desires, aims, aspirations, all of which demand an Object, and imply, by their very existence, that such an Object does exist also'. And so, as Callista finds herself more and more drawn to Christianity as responding 'to all her needs and aspirations', 'the more it seemed . . . to have an external reality and substance'.[53] In the end, the argument from conscience only appears towards the conclusion of the novel, just prior to Callista's conversion.[54]

In one of the finest sermons he ever preached (as an Anglican), 'The Thought of God, the Stay of the Soul' (1837), Newman maintains that one reason why 'God alone is the happiness of our souls' is that

the contemplation of Him, and nothing but it, is able fully to
open and relieve the mind, to unlock ... our affections. ...
Created natures cannot open us ... None but the presence of our
Maker ... for to none besides can the whole heart in all its
thoughts and feelings be unlocked ...

To the Augustinian thought that 'He alone is sufficient for the
heart who made it', it is highly characteristic of Newman to add
the consideration that only God can liberate the human heart by
freeing it from the prison of the self: 'Withdraw the Object on
which it rests, and it will relapse again into its state of confinement and constraint.' Without God, 'We are pent up within ourselves ... we need a relief to our hearts ... that they may not go
on feeding upon themselves; we need to escape from ourselves to
something beyond'.[55]

It would be wrong to attribute all this preoccupation to
Evangelicalism. Subjectivity is one of the most obvious characteristics of Romanticism, and Newman's own sensitivity to the personal and experiential elements in human reasoning can be seen
to belong to a wider movement away from the objectivity and
rationalism of the Enlightenment. But just as he felt that the way
of logic by itself was a cul-de-sac, so also he was only too sensitive
to the danger of turning the propositions of religion into mere expressions of attitude and emotion and imagination. While the
significance of the individual judgement could not be too heavily
emphasized in any credible account of the human mind, on the
other hand it was vitally important not to surrender, like
Schleiermacher, all factual knowledge to science or to abandon
the truth-claims of religion.

The subjectivity, then, that was so pronounced an emphasis of
Newman's thought had to be purified of the egocentric subjectivism that threatened both objectivity and reality. The fear that
one might become the prisoner of one's own feelings and
thoughts was never far from Newman's consciousness while he
was still in the Church of England. To his delighted surprise,
Catholicism provided the key that turned in the lock of this
prison of the self. It is the attempt to give imaginative expression
to this realization that is a prominent feature of his writings
during those post-conversion years when he was discovering
Catholicism.

Notes

1. *The Letters and Diaries of John Henry Newman*, ed. Charles Stephen Dessain *et al.* (London: Nelson, 1961–72; Oxford: Clarendon Press, 1973–), xxiii. 288. Hereafter cit. as *LD*.
2. *LD* v.124.
3. Letter to H. E. Manning, 16 Nov. 1844, cit. Ian Ker, *John Henry Newman: A Biography* (Oxford: Clarendon Press, 1988), 293. Hereafter cit. as Ker.
4. *Apologia pro vita sua*, ed. Martin J. Svaglic (Oxford: Clarendon Press, 1967), 176. Hereafter cit. as *Apo*. See also Ker, 254.
5. *LD* xi.131.
6. *Apo*. 41, 58–9.
7. *LD* iii.227, 230–2, 240–1.
8. *LD* iii.258.
9. *LD* iii.265.
10. *LD* iii.268.
11. *LD* iii.273–4, 227.
12. *LD* iii.277.
13. *LD* iii.280.
14. *LD* iii.289.
15. *Apo*. 43.
16. *Verses on Various Occasions*, 153. All references to Newman's works are to the uniform collected Longmans edition except where otherwise stated.
17. *Certain Difficulties felt by Anglicans in Catholic Teaching*, i.371, 379; ii.24. Hereafter cit. as *Diff.*
18. *LD* xxiv.325.
19. *LD* xi.131.
20. *LD* xi.129.
21. *LD* xi.65, 102; xii.336; xi.146.
22. *LD* xi.252–3.
23. *LD* xii.168.
24. *LD* xi.253.
25. *Discussions and Arguments on Various Subjects*, 388. Hereafter cit. as *DA*.
26. *LD* xii.224.
27. *LD* xii.234.
28. *LD* xxvi.115.
29. See Ker, 364–72.
30. *Present Position of Catholics in England*, 253. Hereafter cit. as *Prepos*.
31. *DA*, 295.
32. *Essays Critical and Historical*, i.313, 333–4; ii.53.
33. Letter to M. Holmes, 6 Sept. 1841, cit. Ker, 230.
34. *Apo*. 40.
35. *Loss and Gain: The Story of a Convert*, 28. Hereafter cit. as *LG*.
36. *Prepos*. 9.
37. *Diff.* i.276, 283.
38. *Diff.* i.284–7.
39. *Diff.* ii.89.
40. Letter to F. Rogers, 10 Jan. 1841, cit. Ker, 191.
41. *LD* xx.220, 339.
42. *Diff.* i.288.
43. *Diff.* i.289–90.
44. *LG* 426–7.
45. *LD* xiv.322.
46. *LD* xxviii.5.
47. *LG* 28.
48. *Great Expectations*, ch. iv.

49. *LG* 327–9.
50. *LG* 427.
51. *Parochial and Plain Sermons*, ii.171 (hereafter cit. as *PS*).
52. *Lectures on the Doctrine of Justification*, 330.
53. *Callista*, 219–20, 265, 292.
54. For a fuller discussion, see Ian Ker, *Healing the Wound of Humanity: The Spirituality of John Henry Newman* (London: Darton, Longman and Todd, 1993), 10–22.
55. *PS* v.316, 318, 324.

4

Metaphor in the Apologia *and Newman's Conversion*

Ronald Begley

I

In the autumn of 1816, as Newman states in the first chapter of the *Apologia pro vita sua*, he read simultaneously two works: Joseph Milner's ecclesiastical history and Thomas Newton's *Dissertations on the Prophecies.*[1]

Newman was deeply moved by the long extracts from Saint Ambrose and Saint Augustine in Milner's history, in which he saw the 'fresh vigorous Power' of the Patristic Church: 'In her triumphant zeal on behalf of that Primeval Mystery, to which I had had so great a devotion from my youth, I recognized the movement of my spiritual Mother. "Incessu patuit Dea."' (*Apo.* 31).

Newman quotes here Virgil's *Aeneid* (I.405). A violent storm had scattered the Trojan fleet. Aeneas and some of his followers arrive on the coast of Africa, whereupon Aeneas and Achates set out to explore. Aeneas's mother Venus appears to him disguised as a young huntress. In response to Aeneas's questions, she tells him where he is, and about the settlement of the area, the ruler Dido, the inhabitants, and their customs. As Venus departs, Aeneas recognizes his mother 'by her step' (*incessu*) and runs after her to reprove her.

Bishop Newton's *Dissertations on the Prophecies*, however, persuaded Newman 'that the Pope was the Antichrist predicted by Daniel, St. Paul, and St. John' (*Apo.* 7). Though Newman does not say so, he evidently shared Newton's view that the papal sceptre was a blunt instrument for smiting the intellect of believers. Newman accordingly defaced his copy of *Gradus ad*

Parnassum by substituting a 'vile' epithet for the traditional papal formula *sceptra gerens,* 'bearing a sceptre' (*Apo.* 120–1). In a celebrated passage Newman writes,

> My imagination was stained by the effects of this doctrine up to the year 1843; it had been obliterated from my reason at an earlier date; but the thought remained upon me as a sort of false conscience. Hence came that conflict of mind, which so many have felt besides myself; – leading some men to make a compromise between two ideas, so inconsistent with each other, – driving others to beat out the one idea or the other from their minds, – and ending in my own case, after many years of intellectual unrest, in the gradual decay and extinction of one of them, – I do not say in its violent death, for why should I not have murdered it sooner, if I murdered it at all? (*Apo.* 7)

We can see the gradual decay and extinction of one of these ideas in Newman's list of the stages in his abandonment of the claim that the Church of Rome was the Antichrist. Newman writes,

> I spoke (successively, but I cannot tell in what order or at what dates) of the Roman Church as being bound up with 'the cause of Antichrist', as being one of the '*many* antichrists' foretold by St. John, as being influenced by 'the *spirit* of Antichrist', and as having something 'very Antichristian' or 'unchristian' about her. (*Apo.* 52)

In the October 1839 number of the *British Critic,* Newman ironically inverts this image by applying to Bishop Newton himself the language of Newton's papal Antichrist and describing Newton as unchurching, banning, smiting, and withering.[2]

I shall be examining Newman's conflict of mind, a related conflict of images, and the gradual decay and extinction of one set of images and its replacement by another. In order to trace this conflict and to describe another kind of inversion, I propose to examine a single paragraph from Newman's *Apologia pro vita sua* – but a very important paragraph, I think, for understanding Newman. I shall examine the passage at length, for the metaphors there shed light on the argument of the passage itself, the argument of the *Apologia* as a whole, and the transformation – so important to Newman's conversion – of the image of the papal weapon which hammers, and thus upon Newman's final appreciation of authority as the guarantee that the Church is a living organism. Before turning to the paragraph itself, however, we need to situate it in its context.

II

Our passage occurs at a climactic moment in what has been described as 'perhaps the most brilliantly subtle of all Newman's writings' and as 'one of the few places where Newman gives anything like a comprehensive account of life and the world': the final chapter of the *Apologia pro vita sua*.[3]

Much of the recent scholarly literature on the last chapter has focused on the covert level of the text, a level at which Newman engages with Liberal Catholics and Ultramontanists over questions about the relation between reason and infallible authority. The evidence about this covert level has been comprehensively documented by Ian Ker, and is sufficiently well known not to require another rehearsal here, except for one point.[4] Döllinger's Munich Congress called for a dialogue between science and theology. Pope Pius IX issued the Munich Brief in March of 1864 and terminated that debate. Shortly thereafter, Acton reluctantly decided to end the *Home and Foreign Review*. Attempting to console Acton, Newman wrote:

> But good may come out of this disappointment. There is life, and increasing life in the English Catholic body; and, if there is life, there must be re-action. It seems impossible that active and sensible men can remain still under the dull tyranny of Manning and Ward.[5]

This remark to Acton is important because it was written in the same year as our passage and, as we shall see, resembles it in its emphasis upon life and upon re-action as a manifestation of life.

In the fifth chapter of the *Apologia* Newman begins by distinguishing between the Catholic creed and system, and, after briefly examining and justifying the Catholic creed (*Apo.* 238–41), he turns to a lengthy examination of the Catholic system, particularly of the infallible authority of the Church. Specifically, Newman asks whether 'the infallible authority' of the Church can, 'with any show of reason, be said in fact to have destroyed the energy of the Catholic intellect' and whether 'the assumption of infallibility by the proper authority is adapted to make me a hypocrite' (*Apo.* 264). Newman undertakes to respond to a 'plausible charge' levelled by Protestant writers that

> I, as a Catholic, not only make profession to hold doctrines which I cannot possibly believe in my heart, but that I also believe in the

existence of a power on earth, which at its own will imposes upon men any new set of *credenda*, when it pleases, by a claim to infallibility; in consequence, that my own thoughts are not my own property; that I cannot tell that tomorrow I may not have to give up what I hold to-day, and that the necessary effect of such a condition of mind must be a degrading bondage, or a bitter inward rebellion relieving itself in secret infidelity, or the necessity of ignoring the whole subject of religion in a sort of disgust, and of mechanically saying everything that the Church says, and leaving to others the defence of it. (*Apo.* 246)

If these Protestant writers are to be believed, a Catholic is 'indifferent' to dogmatic truth, or, 'from a sort of recklessness, will accept any thing that is placed before him', or 'is willing, like a lawyer, to speak according to his brief' (*Apo.* 256).

This is by no means a trivial objection. Neither is it restricted to Protestant writers. Even writers who do not openly embrace this view itself, embrace doctrines implying it. Newman himself had held a similar view, as we shall see shortly. And the issue was a matter of intense controversy among English Catholics in the period immediately preceding the composition of the *Apologia*.

We are now ready to quote the paragraph in question (*Apo.* 251–2). To facilitate reference, I have numbered the sentences in the paragraph.

(1) All this being considered as the profession which I make *ex animo*, as for myself, so also on the part of the Catholic body, as far as I know it, it will at first sight be said that the restless intellect of our common humanity is utterly weighed down, to the repression of all independent effort and action whatever, so that, if this is to be the mode of bringing it into order, it is brought into order only to be destroyed. (2) But this is far from the result, far from what I conceive to be the intention of that high Providence who has provided a great remedy for a great evil, – far from borne out by the history of the conflict between Infallibility and Reason in the past, and the prospect of it in the future. (3) The energy of the human intellect 'does from opposition grow'; it thrives and is joyous, with a tough elastic strength, under the terrible blows of the divinely-fashioned weapon, and is never so much itself as when it has lately been overthrown. (4) It is the custom with Protestant writers to consider that, whereas there are two great principles in action in the history of religion, Authority and Private Judgment, they have all the Private Judgment to themselves, and we have the full inheritance and the superincumbent oppression of Authority. (5) But this is not so; it is the vast

Catholic body itself, and it only, which affords an arena for both combatants in that awful, never-dying duel. (6) It is necessary for the very life of religion, viewed in its large operations and its history, that the warfare should be incessantly carried on. (7) Every exercise of Infallibility is brought out into act by an intense and varied operation of the Reason, both as its ally and as its opponent, and provokes again, when it has done its work, a reaction of Reason against it; and, as in a civil polity the State exists and endures by means of the rivalry and collision, the encroachments and defeats of its constituent parts, so in like manner Catholic Christendom is no simple exhibition of religious absolutism, but presents a continuous picture of Authority and Private Judgment alternately advancing and retreating as the ebb and flow of the tide; – it is a vast assemblage of human beings with wilful intellects and wild passions, brought together into one by the beauty and the Majesty of a Superhuman Power, – into what may be called a large reformatory or training-school, not as if into a hospital or into a prison, not in order to be sent to bed, not to be buried alive, but (if I may change my metaphor) brought together as if into some moral factory, for the melting, refining, and moulding, by an incessant, noisy process, of the raw material of human nature, so excellent, so dangerous, so capable of divine purposes.

Newman maintains, as Ian Ker observes, that 'far from being mutually contradictory, authority and reason need each other precisely because, paradoxically, each is actually sustained by conflict with the other'.[6] This view places Newman at odds with Protestant writers who maintain that Catholic Christendom is an 'exhibition of religious absolutism' and that Catholics 'have the full inheritance and the superincumbent oppression of Authority' (*Apo.* 252, sentence 7; sentence 4).

The view Newman attributes to 'Protestant writers' (*Apo.* 252, sentence 4) applies, for instance, to Charles Kingsley's review of J. A. Froude's *History of England* in *Macmillan's Magazine* – the review in which Kingsley made his charges of dishonesty against Newman – as well as to Froude's history. It also applies to Newman's Anglican writings, for he had written,

> Rome ... maintains that nothing is absolutely left to individual judgment; that is, that there is no subject in religious faith and conduct on which the Church may not pronounce a decision, such as to supersede the private judgment, and compel the assent, of every one of her members.[7]

It is clear therefore that our paragraph has a good deal to do with the 'intellectual unrest' (*Apo.* 7) of Newman the Anglican and with a fundamental issue of his conversion.

The seven sentences composing our paragraph are a meticulously crafted whole. The main pattern stands clear. First a claim that the bringing to order in the Catholic Church is such as to preclude life (*Apo.* 251, sentence 1); next, a two-sentence rebuttal introduced by an adversative (*Apo.* 251–2, sentences 2 and 3); then a second denial of life to the Catholic Church (*Apo.* 252, sentence 4); followed by another two-sentence rebuttal, introduced by the same adversative (*Apo,* 252, sentences 5 and 6); and, finally, a capping periodic sentence. As Catholic Christendom, according to Newman (*Apo.* 252, sentence 7), presents 'a continuous picture of Authority and Private Judgment alternately advancing and retreating as the ebb and flow of the tide', so Protestant claims and Catholic rebuttals 'advance' and 'retreat' in Newman's paragraph.

After the ebb and flow and the 'advance' and 'retreat', the shortest sentence in our passage comes as a kind of climax. There Newman makes what is, I think, the central claim of the passage: that 'incessant' warfare is 'necessary for the very life of religion' (*Apo.* 252, sentence 6).

This climactic short sentence is thrown into relief by the last sentence – which is, with its 205 words, one of the longest in the *Apologia*. There Newman is engaging so many claims, rebuttals, actions, persons and images at once that his syntax is strained to its limits. Newman rejects four metaphors of the Church, then appears to settle upon two new metaphors, only to abandon them suddenly and to 'change' his 'metaphor' by likening the Church to a 'moral factory'. By postponing the metaphor and referring parenthetically to the change of metaphor, Newman focuses our attention upon it. In a chapter in which, as Holloway asserts, every metaphor 'means more than one thinks at first glance', one would be hard-pressed to find a more carefully prepared metaphor.[8] Newman is neither 'mechanically saying everything that the Church says' (*Apo.* 246), nor speaking 'according to his brief' (*Apo.* 256), but dramatizing the conflict within himself to appropriate the mystery of the Church more actively.

With a few carefully-chosen details, Newman evokes the picture of a metalworker shaping a piece of metal by hammering it with a 'divinely-fashioned weapon' (*Apo.* 252, sentence 3). Just before our paragraph, Newman had prepared the metaphor by describing the infallible authority of the Church as 'a working instrument ... for smiting hard and throwing back the immense energy of the aggressive, capricious, untrustworthy intellect' (*Apo.* 245–6). On the face of it Newman is describing the oldest metal-working process: the shaping of pure iron by hammering.[9]

Among the details of the hammering Newman places particular emphasis on the 'tough elastic strength' of the human mind (*Apo.* 252, sentence 3). Newman uses the term 'elastic' to denote the property identified in a recent dictionary of physics as one whereby 'a solid material changes its shape and size under the action of opposing forces, but recovers its original configuration when the forces are removed'.[10] After sustaining a certain amount of stress a solid reaches and exceeds its elastic limit and thereupon undergoes permanent deformation.

There is another, no less crucial dimension to this sentence. Though Newman undoubtedly means to speak for Catholic Christians generally, his words bear directly on himself. I quoted earlier from Newman's letter to Acton in which he professes to see signs of life and re-action among English Catholics to the 'dull tyranny' of Ward and Manning. We have here, I think, Newman's life-manifesting, elastic 're-action' to a 'violent ultra party, which exalts opinions into dogmas' (*Apo.* 260).[11] As Newman writes in our paragraph, 'Every exercise of Infallibility is brought out into act by an intense and varied operation of the Reason, both as its ally and as its opponent, and provokes again, when it has done its work, a re-action of Reason against it' (*Apo.* 252, sentence 7).

Newman now describes Catholic Christendom as a 'vast assemblage' brought together 'as if into some moral factory, for the melting, refining, and moulding, by an incessant, noisy process, of the raw material of human nature' (*Apo.* 252, sentence 7). After numerous delays he returns strikingly to the basic imagistic pattern we have seen in sentence 3. Newman's parenthetical remark about his 'change' of metaphor notwithstanding (*Apo.* 252, sentence 7), Newman returns and develops the earlier metaphor – indeed, I would argue, he is developing and transforming the image of hammering which can be traced back to the autumn of 1816.

The mention of melting, refining and moulding likewise adds an important element to the developing picture. Newman now metaphorically identifies the conflict between human reason and infallible authority with the process of casting or founding, the shaping of metal by melting and pouring it into a mould.[12] As he earlier displayed an accurate knowledge of the process of forging, of the strength of materials, and of stresses and strains, so here

Newman writes accurately about the casting of metals. Several pure metals are insufficiently ductile or rust too easily. For centuries craftsmen have overcome these disadvantages by combining, for example, copper and tin to produce bronze – which is stronger and harder than either of its constituents.[13]

Newman is describing, then, the relation of infallible authority to reason in terms of an idealized vision of a craftsman in metal. The actual details of the metallurgical metaphor do more than merely convey an atmosphere or illustrate the argument, however. The unexpectedness and persistence of the metaphor prompt us to consider its source. As we inspect the passage more closely, it seems to me, the craftsman comes into sharper focus, and he proves to be not a vague figure, but a particular person in particular circumstances – and one moving in a dense atmosphere of implication. The particular person is the Lord of Fire and master metalworker, Vulcan, as he appears in Virgil's *Aeneid* (VIII, 370–453, 608–731). Of this passage, Edmund Burke has said he doubts whether there is any in the entire *Aeneid* 'more grand' and 'laboured'.[14]

The circumstances are as follows. Aeneas is making preparations for his final conflict with Turnus. Aeneas's mother Venus asks Vulcan to make armour for her son. Vulcan 'promises full satisfaction – the utmost that iron and molten alloys can produce' (VIII, 403). Before dawn Vulcan visits his smithy, a volcanic cave under Sicily's Mount Etna (VIII, 416–24) where 'fire pants in the furnace' (VIII, 421). Vulcan finds there his three 'strikers', the Cyclops, at work upon other projects. Vulcan orders them to interrupt these projects and to forge and cast Aeneas's shield (VIII, 439–43) with hammers and metal-twisting tongs (VIII, 451–3) upon anvils.

Virgil brings home the smoke, fire, and, above all, the hammering. In Virgil's description of the hammering (VIII, 452–3), for example, the striking and unusual metrical pattern there, as R. D. Williams observes, conveys 'heavy and difficult movement' – as if to emphasize Vulcan's struggle with the resisting raw material.[15]

The images on the surface of the shield represent warfare which is 'incessantly carried on' (cf. *Apo.* 252, sentence 6) and the shield itself is the product of an 'incessant, noisy process' (cf. *Apo.* 252, sentence 7). Vulcan makes the various layers of the shield into a living unity (*non enarrabile textum*, VIII, 625).

Vulcan not only melts, refines, and moulds alloys into a unity, but he also arranges and unifies the sculpted images which decorate the surface of the shield. The main theme of those images is the wars the Romans will fight as they build their vast empire (*pugnataque in ordine bella*, VIII, 629). Vulcan includes scenes from early Roman history, and on the three-part central panel he represents the battle of Actium and the triple triumph of Augustus – which ushered in the *pax Augusta*.

Virgil emphasizes the virtuosity of the divine craftsman, who can convey emotion (VIII, 649–50) and give life and movement to the metal shield, as when, for example, he represents dolphins playing (VIII, 671–4).

Aeneas rejoices in the images affixed to the shield, but he is ignorant of what the images represent (*miratur rerumque ignarus imagine gaudet*, VIII, 730). He lifts on to his shoulders, as one commentator observes, 'in actuality the pictured shield of Vulcan, but metaphorically the future destiny of Rome'.[16]

The Virgilian provenance of the metaphor may initially surprise us. On the other hand, Newman alludes to the *Aeneid* with sophistication elsewhere in the *Apologia*, as, for example, in the reference to Aeneas's encounter with the disguised Venus that I quoted earlier (*Apo.* 31), and in an intricate and wide-ranging allusion to Aeneas's account of the fall of Troy at the beginning of Chapter Three (*Apo.* 92–3). And we cannot rule out the possibility that Newman had theological considerations for alluding to Virgil at this climactic point, for, as he had observed earlier, 'pagan literature, philosophy and mythology, properly understood, were but a preparation for the Gospel' (*Apo.* 27).

But what is the significance of Newman's allusion? Symbolically, at least, the Church is like Vulcan's shield, for both have a dual aspect of defensive weapon and image. The Church is a defensive weapon and possesses 'the force and the toughness necessary to be a breakwater against the deluge' (*Apo.* 244). Like the shield, moreover, the Church is the product of an 'incessant, noisy process'. Like the shield, the Church is an image and 'will remain', Newman writes, 'even to the end of the world, after all but a symbol of those heavenly facts which fill eternity' (*Apo.* 27). In forming an empire whose 'indefinite extension' and 'unlimited duration' Christ announced, the Church calls to mind the imperial images on the surface of the shield.[17] Finally and perhaps most importantly, both the Church and Vulcan's shield are images which possess life and movement.

It has been observed that Newman's characteristic way of expounding Christianity is to show

that the Church is a system of persons and rituals and customs, a
single real thing, not an abstract theory; and this he tends to do
in two stages. First, a vivid impression of the multifariousness,
energy, and incessant changes of human life everywhere on earth
runs through most of his work. ... Then in contrast, he suggests
how in the Catholic Church this variety and energy are not cur-
tailed, but effortlessly and beautifully coordinated, until every aspect of human life finds its place there in an incomparable order.[18]

It is very striking that the same point has been made about
Vulcan's shield:

when the attributes of Vulcan are combined with those of Venus,
the result is the channeling of energy into a pattern of order
wherein fire is forced to mold the armor of a heroism strong but
reasoned.[19]

There can be no doubt that Newman knew Virgil's epic thoroughly. He studied the work as an undergraduate and young don,
and visited Virgil's grave during his Mediterranean cruise of
1832–3.[20]

During that Mediterranean cruise, Newman took two trips to
Sicily. The second trip took place in the spring of 1833. He travelled there, he writes, 'for the gratification of an imagination, for
the idea of a warm fancy', drawn 'by a strange love of Sicily to
gaze upon its cities and mountains'.[21] The imagination Newman
sought to gratify was in large measure his Classical imagination.
He was eager, for example, to compare Thucydides's account of
the Sicilian expedition from *The History of the Peloponnesian War*
to the Sicilian terrain.

It is also clear that Newman particularly desired to gaze upon
Mount Etna. Newman walked to the foot of Mount Etna from
Taormina and would have climbed it, if he had not been pre-
vented by snow. We know, moreover, that he had a copy of
Virgil's *Aeneid* with him.[22] Though nothing can be proved,
nothing is easier to imagine than that he 'realized' and dwelt upon
Virgil's description of Vulcan's smithy and of the forging of
Aeneas's shield as he stood at the foot of Mount Etna.

This possibility is strengthened, it seems to me, by the consideration that Newman echoes his account of his trip to Sicily in
our paragraph from the last chapter of the *Apologia*. Newman
states that the 'energy of the human intellect ... thrives and is joyous, with a tough elastic strength, under the terrible blows of the
divinely-fashioned weapon' (*Apo.* 252, sentence 3). This calls to

mind the passage in which Newman describes his 'exuberant and joyous energy' upon his return from Sicily, an exultation of 'health restored' and 'home regained' (*Apo.* 43).

III

The metaphor in our paragraph has other sources besides Virgil. A typological image of the building of the temple of Solomon runs in symbolic tandem with the smithing of Aeneas's shield. In order to deepen our understanding of the conflict between Milner and Newton in Newman's mind as well as of our paragraph, we must now examine a passage in the *Essay on Development* where the tension between reason and infallible authority is clearly portrayed, and where, appropriately, the discussion centres on an image of hammering, casting and moulding.

Newman is examining the historical evidence for the papal supremacy in the early Church and he makes two main points: that 'the papal development could hardly be expected to show itself in the conditions of the first three centuries of church life' and 'that, as more favourable conditions developed in the fourth and fifth centuries, no one could fail to discern clearly the growth and existence of the papal polity'.[23] When 'the power of the Holy See began to exert itself', Newman observes, the 'necessary consequence' of this was 'disturbance and collision'. In the course of his analysis, Newman writes:

> Of the Temple of Solomon it was said that 'neither hammer, nor axe, nor any tool or iron was heard in the house, while it was in building'. This is a type of the Church above; it was otherwise with the Church below, whether in the instance of Popes or Apostles.[24]

When Solomon had his temple built, we recall, eighty thousand stoneworkers 'quarried out great costly stones in order to lay the foundation of the house with dressed stones' (1 Kings 5.15; 1 Kings 5.17). Hiram sent from Tyre a master craftsman named Huram-abi, a man skilled in 'gold, silver, bronze, iron, stone and wood' (2 Chron. 2.13–14). Newman emphasizes the fact that the craftsmen cut, shaped, and prepared all the stones not at the sacred site but at the quarry (1 Kings 6.7). They were probably observing the deuteronomic prohibitions against the use of iron tools in constructing an altar (Deut. 27.5; Josh. 8.31).

For our purposes here the important points about the passage in Newman's *Essay on Development* are: first, that while the Church above is characterized by silence, the Church below is characterized by 'disturbance and collision', particularly by 'conflict between Infallibility and Reason' (cf. *Apo.* 251, sentence 2); and secondly, that Newman understands the 'disturbance and collision' between St Cyprian and Pope Stephen, between Polycrates and St Victor, between Leo and the Monophysites as evidence of the life of the Church.[25]

In a number of respects, then, Newman's passage in the *Essay* parallels our paragraph from the concluding chapter of the *Apologia*. Here we have a process very like the building of the shield by Vulcan. In both texts we have hammering, casting and moulding. As Vulcan stands to the passage from the *Aeneid*, so the master craftsman Huram-abi stands to the building of Solomon's temple. Most importantly, the incessant noise in the 'Church below' contrasts with the silence of the building of the Temple of Solomon and of the Church Above, but parallels the 'incessant, noisy process' of the 'melting, refining, and moulding' in the Church's 'moral factory' (*Apo.* 252, sentence 7).

In our paragraph, I submit, the temple image and the shield image grow together into a fresh unity. As Newman prepares the shield image by introducing the theme of hammering before our paragraph, so he prepares the temple image by writing that the Church teaches 'that each individual man must be in his own person one whole and perfect temple of God, while he is also one of the living stones which build up a visible religious community' (*Apo.* 248).

IV

The foregoing analysis of a single paragraph from the *Apologia pro vita sua* has been conducted through a hypothetical reconstruction of the process by which it was generated, beginning with the 'intellectual unrest' of the autumn of 1816. In offering the analysis my purpose has been twofold: to clarify the relevance of Newman's metaphor to his train of thought, and, more broadly, to suggest how this type of analysis can shed light on the imaginative dimension of Newman's conversion and on the concrete being that reasons. I am using the term 'conversion' here in Newman's sense, as the process, not the commencement of a religious course – the gradual changing, not an initial change ... Every baptized person is under a process of divine influence and sanctification, a process often interrupted, often given over, then resumed, irregularly carried on, heartily entered into, finally completed as the case may be.[26]

Our paragraph contains the core of Newman's 'General Answer to Mr. Kingsley' – as the final chapter of the *Apologia* was entitled in the first edition of 1864. Not coincidentally, it also contains what Ian Ker describes as 'Newman's fundamental reason ... for converting to the Roman Catholic Church': 'the argument from development, and consequently the argument from authority'.[27]

If an idea like that of Christianity is to be a living idea, it must evidence development. But developments have to be distinguished from corruptions, and although Newman did indeed offer seven 'Tests' or 'Notes' ... this did not remove the need for a living authority to pronounce on the legitimacy of the developments in question.[28]

The key claim in our paragraph is this: 'It is necessary for the very life of religion, viewed in its large operations and its history, that the warfare should be incessantly carried on' (*Apo.* 252, sentence 6). The operative word in that sentence is 'life'. Developments in doctrine – the vital sign of a living Church – are brought about by the collisions between a living authority and the 'restless' operations of Reason, so that, contrary to the claims of a Kingsley, the individual intellect is not 'buried alive' under the weight of Catholic authority, but 'thrives and is joyous' (*Apo.* 251–2, sentence 1, sentence 7, sentence 3).

On the face of it, it seems very strange that Newman would choose a factory for the climactic metaphor in a passage arguing that the Church is a unity of living intelligences. Elsewhere Newman favours organic metaphors for the Church, likening it to the world of Nature or the human body.[29] The images of a factory and a hammering craftsman would appear to be mechanical metaphors, working against the idea of a living Church. If my central contentions here carry conviction, however, we can now see that the image of the metalworking craftsman had been practically Newman's own since 1816 and that there was a deep appropriateness in Newman's selection of it.

I have tried to show, in the first place, that the image of the 'divinely-fashioned weapon' in our paragraph calls to mind a

Newtonian papal Antichrist using his sceptre as a blunt weapon. As the argument that the Church of Rome changed was initially an objection to that Church but ultimately a sign of its divine provenance, so the image of the figure with the sceptre becomes a craftsman with a hammer: the negative features fade and the positive become prominent. Newman's description of Pope Leo I illustrates this point. Referring to his studies (during the summer of 1839) of the Monophysite controversy and the conduct of Leo at Chalcedon, Newman writes, 'Down had come the *Via Media* as a definite theory or scheme, under the blows of St. Leo' (*Apo.* 120). Bishop Newton's papal Antichrist had undergone a transformation and acquired a positive aspect.

I have suggested further that the hammering craftsman is Virgil's Vulcan and that the factory is the smithy under Mount Etna which we see in *Aeneid* VIII. There, in the noise and hissing of hammering and moulding, the divine craftsman brings into a unity on Aeneas's shield the varied elements of the life and history of Rome. His craft is so great that the resulting scenes have life and movement, and much of the movement is the conflict of battle, like Newman's 'warfare . . . incessantly carried on' in the living Church. When we add to the Virgilian allusion the hint of the building of Solomon's temple, we have by contrast further emphasis on the noise and collision in the life of the Church below. Thus Newman's climactic metaphor is not (say) the Soho Manufactory of Birmingham, but an image of the life-giving work of Authority on Reason, accompanied by the noise of their unending warfare.

Newman is not 'mechanically saying everything that the Church says' (*Apo.* 246). Neither is his metaphor mechanical. On the contrary, Newman brings out 'in a substantive form' a living Church, 'made of flesh and blood, with voice, complexion, and motion and action, and a will of its own' (*Apo.* 72). In other words, Newman recognizes his Spiritual Mother by her step (*Apo.* 31). The Virgilian quotation in Chapter One (*Apo.* 31) sustains the Virgilian allusion in our paragraph. But this recognition differs from that which took place in the autumn of 1816 in one crucial respect. Newman now realizes that his Spiritual Mother's 'step' is, metaphorically, her doctrinal, dogmatic, and theological development. Newman's living intelligence neither murders nor beats Bishop Newton's idea out of his mind. In the Virgilian and Scriptural image of our paragraph, Newman's living intelligence encounters the living idea of Catholic Christianity.

In a celebrated passage of the *Grammar of Assent*, Newman invites us to consider 'how differently young and old are affected by the words of some classic author' such as Homer, Horace, or Virgil:

> Passages, which to a boy are but rhetorical commonplaces, neither better nor worse than a hundred others which any clever writer might supply, which he gets by heart and thinks very fine, and imitates, as he thinks, successfully, in his own flowing versification, at length come home to him, when long years have passed, and he has had experience of life, and pierce him, as if he had never before known them, with their sad earnestness and vivid exactness.[30]

As Newman composed our passage in the *Apologia*, I suggest, Virgil's lines about the forging of Aeneas's shield pierced him, 'as if he had never before known them', with their 'vivid exactness'.

After years of 'intellectual unrest', after long isolation from former Tractarians, after collisions with the bishops during his editorship of the *Rambler*, after the Munich Brief, after protracted disagreements with the Ultramontanists and liberal Catholics over reason and authority, after the whole 'incessant, noisy process', Newman has not exceeded his limit of elasticity. On the contrary, he displays the exultation of 'health restored' and 'home regained' (*Apo.* 43).

Notes

1. Unless otherwise noted, all references to Newman's works will be to the Uniform Edition of his works, prepared by Newman during his lifetime. We shall use the standard abbreviations listed in volume II of *The Letters and Diaries of John Henry Newman* (31 vols.; ed. C. S. Dessain *et al.*; vols 1–6, Oxford: Clarendon Press, 1978–84; vols 11–22, London: Nelson, 1961–72; vols 23–31, Oxford: Clarendon Press, 1973–7). Hereafter all references to the *Apologia pro vita sua* will be placed in the text. *Apo.* 6–7.
2. *Ess.*, vol. 2, 138–9.
3. Ian Ker, *John Henry Newman: A Biography* (Oxford: Oxford University Press, 1988), 550; John Holloway, *The Victorian Sage: Studies in Argument* (London: Norton, 1988), 291.
4. See, for example, Ker, *John Henry Newman*, 549–59.
5. *LD*, vol. 21, 84. For a full discussion of this incident see Ker, *John Henry Newman*, 541.
6. Ker, *John Henry Newman*, 551–2.
7. *VM*, I, 128.
8. Holloway, *The Victorian Sage*, 291.
9. On the shaping of iron by hammering see Percy Knauth, *The Metalsmiths* (New York: Time-Life Books, 1974), 82–96.
10. Daniel Lapedes, ed., *McGraw Hill Dictionary of Physics and Mathematics* (New York: McGraw-Hill, 1978), 296–7.
11. Ker, *John Henry Newman*, 554.
12. For forging and casting see Knauth, *The Metalsmiths*, 48–9, 114–15.

13. On alloys see Knauth, *The Metalsmiths*, 55–7.
14. Edmund Burke, *A Philosophical Inquiry into the Origin of our Ideas of the Sublime and Beautiful* (New York: Harper, 1844), 211.
15. R. D. Williams, *The Aeneid*, 2 vols (London: Macmillan, 1972), vol. 2, 258.
16. Williams, *The Aeneid*, vol. 2, 276.
17. *PS*, vol. 2, 245. In this passage, Newman is applying to the Church Jupiter's prophecy to Venus about the Romans: *His ego nec metas rerum, nec tempora pono: Imperium sine fine dedi*. For Newman's 'imperial' image of the Church see Paul Misner, *Papacy and Development: Newman and the Primacy of the Pope* (Leiden: E. J. Brill, 1976), 50–7.
18. Holloway, *The Victorian Sage*, 177.
19. Michael Putnam, *The Poetry of the Aeneid* (Ithaca: Cornell University Press, 1988), 141.
20. For Newman's studies in Virgil's *Aeneid* see Sheridan Gilley, *Newman and his Age* (Westminster, Md.: Christian Classics, 1991), 30, 44.
21. *AW*, 11.
22. *LD*, vol. 3, 303–4; Ker, *John Henry Newman*, 75. For Newman's possession of a copy of Virgil with him in Sicily see *AW*, 135; Meriol Trevor, *Pillar of the Cloud* (Garden City, N.Y.: Doubleday, 1962), 126.
23. Misner, *Papacy and Development*, 92.
24. *Dev.*, 152.
25. *Dev.*, 152.
26. Unpublished manuscript of Newman, A.91: 'Remarks on the Covenant of Grace, in connection with the Doctrines of Election, Baptism and the Church' (1828). Quoted in William Fey, 'Development of Doctrine and the Spiritual Development of the Believer', *Louvain Studies* 15 (1990), 166–87, esp. 176.
27. Ian Ker, *Newman and the Fullness of Christianity* (Edinburgh: T. & T. Clark, 1993), 115.
28. *Ibid.*
29. See the examples cited in Holloway, *Victorian Sage*, 183.
30. *GA*, 78.

5

Newman and Kierkegaard on the Act of Faith

John Macquarrie

Nineteenth-century Europe must be one of the most complex and even tangled epochs in human history. The eighteenth century we call the 'Age of Reason', and to say that someone was a typical eighteenth-century thinker would suggest to our minds the fairly definite image of a person committed to the ideals of the Enlightenment. But the nineteenth century was too pluralistic for us to be able to form the image of a typical nineteenth-century thinker.

It might be said that we are too ready to type or even stereotype figures of the past, overlooking the unique combination of qualities to be found in each. We have a great range of labels that we are ready to stick on to people; 'rationalist', 'empiricist', 'romanticist' and so on almost indefinitely, but these adjectives tell us little and may even be misleading. Yet when we try to understand what was going on, we cannot help engaging in some typing and classifying. This will do no harm provided that we understand that there are no labels that fit exactly and exhaustively, and no people who conform wholly to the typological scheme we have set up. In each individual different characteristics are combined in a unique way, and we have to pay as much attention to the differences between that individual and another person as to the similarities between them. This *caveat* is especially important in our present task of exploring possible comparisons between Newman and Kierkegaard. We shall find points of resemblance but also marked differences that would make it impossible to classify Newman as an existentialist or to assert that

Kierkegaard, if he had lived longer, would have been converted to Roman Catholicism.

In his history of religious thought in nineteenth-century Britain, Bernard Reardon says of Newman: 'He is, probably, the outstanding religious figure of his century, with the sole exception of Kierkegaard, a man of whom he himself had probably never heard.'[1] Newman, we suppose, had never heard of Kierkegaard partly because of the insularity of English theology, partly because, as Reardon points out, both Newman and Kierkegaard were very much undervalued in their own time, and only in the twentieth century has their true worth been recognized. Even so, we may be surprised that Reardon has elevated these two men to the highest rank among the religious figures of their century. Neither of them was a theologian or philosopher of religion in the narrower technical sense. But both of them were religious thinkers of great originality, and when we take into account the influence which they have exercised and still exercise, then we shall not simply dismiss the claim that Reardon makes for them.

The most obvious link between the two men is that in matters of religion, there are questions which cannot be settled by reason alone, and that we may admit a specifically religious insight into the conclusions which we reach on these questions. Both Newman and Kierkegaard are agreed that faith is somehow independent of reason. This may seem to make faith more vulnerable, for no rational proof can be given of the reality of faith's object. But, on the other hand, the person who has faith has no need of any rational demonstration, for such a person has, in his or her experience, a direct awareness of the object of faith and this awareness brings its own certitude, so that any 'proof' would be superfluous or even unsettling.

If we return for a moment to look again at the tangled thicket of nineteenth-century thought, we can see a continuous line running through it, and both Newman and Kierkegaard are situated on that line, though in different ways. The line may be described as a challenge to the omnicompetence of reason. In the earlier phases of the Enlightenment, it was believed that reason could encompass even God, and that natural theology, based on reason alone, could discover all the fundamental religious truths that had been taught on the basis of the Bible. The classic example was the book *De Veritate*, by Edward, Lord Herbert of Cherbury, which established on rational grounds five basic beliefs: there exists a Supreme Being, we have a duty to worship him, true worship consists in a life of virtue, we have a duty to repent of our sins, and there will be a future life bringing both rewards and punishments. But when, in 1793, Kant published his *Religion within the Limits of Reason Alone*, the situation had changed. In spite of the title of the book, faith was no longer founded on reason but was given a sphere of its own alongside reason. As Kant himself had expressed it in an earlier work, his aim was 'to deny knowledge in order to make room for faith'.[2] Belief in God was now said to rest not on rational demonstration but on the demands of our moral nature. God is a postulate of the moral life. Six years after Kant, Schleiermacher's *Speeches on Religion* shifted the seat of religious faith to the affective nature of the human being. Religion, he maintained, is primarily neither a matter of the intellect nor of the will but of the feelings. In his later writings, it became the 'feeling of absolute dependence'.[3] Such a feeling is for Schleiermacher also an intuition, that is to say, it is not just a subjective emotion but an actual apprehension of the object of faith. Thus we find him saying that the feeling of absolute dependence takes the place of the traditional proofs of God's existence.[4] So already at the beginning of the nineteenth century, and long before either Newman or Kierkegaard were writing, some thinkers with religious interests were trying to find a basis for faith that would deliver it from dependence on reason. But whereas in the case of Kant the new basis was to be sought in the will and the claims of morality, in Schleiermacher the move was towards feeling, though a feeling that apparently has some cognitive power.

At first sight, it may seem easiest to relate Kierkegaard to these earlier nineteenth-century thinkers. On the other hand, it is never easy to understand Kierkegaard or to see exactly what he is doing. We find him saying: 'the highest pitch of every passion is always to will its own downfall; and so it is also the supreme passion of the Reason to seek a collision, though this collision must in one way or another prove its undoing.'[5] What does this mean? Reason has or is itself a passion? Reason seeks its own downfall, therefore it seeks a collision? A possible interpretation may be something as follows. For Kierkegaard, human experience is a whole, and our tendency to break up experience into knowing, feeling, willing and whatever else we may think appropriate is an artificial procedure. Reason is not detached, judicious, value-free as some epistemologists used to claim. Reason is always motivated by some desire or passion, it is never detached from the complete person, who does not so much exercise reason, as if that were some tool

that could be taken up or laid down, but rather exercises itself as
rational. Similarly a human person (except perhaps in pathologi-
cal cases) is never swept along by mindless passion but is also in
some degree governed by intellect and by conscious will. Reason
seeks a collision, even its downfall, if it is, so to speak, thinned
down, reduced, alienated one might almost say, from the total humanity of the person to whom that reason belongs, and perhaps
something like that happens when reason seeks to be totally
value-free. Then, alienated from its integral place in the totality of
the person, it will indeed seek its own downfall, by seeking to re-
establish its connection with those areas of the unitary self from
which the attempt has been made to cut it off. This may be what
Kierkegaard has in mind in his vivid metaphor of 'seeking a collision'. The assumption behind it is that the basic human passion
is the quest for God, the Augustinian idea that our hearts are restless till they find rest in God. Reason does not find God, for God
is beyond the reach of reason. But reason, so to speak, shatters itself against God. Let us hear Kierkegaard's words at this point:

> The paradoxical passion of the Reason thus comes repeatedly into
> collision with the Unknown, which does indeed exist, but is un-
> known, and in so far does not exist. The Reason cannot advance
> beyond this point, and yet it cannot refrain in its paradoxicalness
> from arriving at this limit and occupying itself therewith. It will
> not serve to dismiss its relation to it simply by asserting that the
> Unknown does not exist, since this itself involves a relationship.
> But what then is the Unknown, since the designation of it as God
> merely signifies for us that it is unknown? To say that it is the
> Unknown because it cannot be known, and even if it were capable
> of being known, it could not be expressed, does not satisfy the de-
> mands of passion, though it correctly interprets the Unknown as
> a limit; but a limit is precisely a torment for passion, though it
> also serves as an incitement. And yet the Reason can come no
> further, whether it risks a way out by the *via negationis* or *via
> eminentiae*.[6]

I shall not quote further, but it is at this impasse that a decision, an act of will, is demanded. One either makes the leap of
faith, or one takes offence and turns away. But how is the leap of
faith possible? For Kierkegaard, the answer to that question is
'revelation'. In the incarnation, God has come among us in the
form of a servant, and made himself accessible. Reason comes to
a halt before the Unknown, but the Unknown makes himself
known to faith. Is the leap of faith then something quite

arbitrary? Kierkegaard does indeed say that one is not brought to the place where the leap takes place by a build-up of probabilities, as if reason could bring us so far by natural theology, and then we add revelation as a kind of coping stone. The revelation itself is the supreme paradox, the paradox of the God-man, which for reason is an absurdity. No kind of natural knowledge can help at this point. Thus Kierkegaard is also negative in his attitude to history and historical knowledge. No amount of detailed knowledge about the earthly life of Jesus could ever bring us to the point at which we would confess, 'This man is God with us'. All historical knowledge is of a different order from what we learn in faith. There seems to be a sharp discontinuity between the two. Indeed, even for those who accept the revelation, there is much that remains unknown or inexpressible. David Law, in his recent study *Kierkegaard as Negative Theologian*, remarks, 'We overcome uncertainty by making a decision to construct our lives on an acceptance of the disputed proposition, despite its uncertainty.'[7]

One is reminded here of Pascal's famous wager, and again the question of arbitrariness arises. But Pascal also spoke of a 'logic of the heart' of which, he claimed, reason knows nothing. Is there some kind of spiritual perception or discernment at work here, a discernment to which, for those to whom it is given, perceptions of material reality are far inferior? As we have noted, Kierkegaard believes that even the Christian revelation leaves much that is either unknown or unsayable. But he insists strongly that it says as much as we need to know – enough, that is, for life.

Kierkegaard goes so far as to declare:

> If the contemporary generation had left nothing behind them but these words: 'We have believed that in such and such a year God has appeared among us in the humble figure of a servant, that he lived and taught in our community, and finally died', it would be more than enough.[8]

I do not think we can agree with him at this point. Even if he is right in thinking that the multiplication of historical details concerning Jesus would never reveal his Christhood, surely we need to know something more than the bare facts in Kierkegaard's statement. Certainly he makes a central point – that God appeared in servant form – but must we not know also some of the things that were done in this servant form, some of the teaching that was given, something more about the end of this life beyond the bare 'he finally died'? The gospels do not give us what would be reckoned a full biography of Jesus, but they do tell us enough to let us form a coherent picture. Can we really accept that the gospels might as well never have been written? Could we get by on, say, the letters of Paul which have plenty of spiritual insight into the significance of Christ for faith but only a very few scattered allusions to the history of Jesus?

We may agree with Kierkegaard that to have faith in Jesus as the Christ demands more than factual information. It needs spiritual insight – a phrase which is taken from Paul, who writes: 'The unspiritual man does not receive the gifts of the Spirit of God, for they are folly to him, and he is not able to understand them because they are spiritually discerned' (1 Cor. 2.14). So how do we ever come to the faith that discerns Christ where knowledge fails? Is this alleged spiritual discernment of Jesus as the Christ something quite different from the actual physical perception of him available to his contemporaries, or the imaginative perception of Jesus as a historical being available to us on reading the gospel narratives? Clearly the two cannot be entirely separate unless Jesus Christ is two separate beings, as I suppose he might possibly be represented in some kind of Nestorian heresy run riot – though we may doubt that anyone, even Nestorius himself, has ever entertained such views. But just as a human being is more than a physical organism and is in fact a *person*, endowed with thought, freedom, perception, will, purpose, and all the other properties that belong to a person, so even the physical perception of a person is normally accompanied by a 'reading' of his action and speech that involves a reconstruction through 'empathy' or whatever word we may employ of the thoughts, feelings, purposes etc. which the person is experiencing.

Now, perhaps Kierkegaard did come pretty close to separating the Christ from the historical or human Jesus, for he does speak of the Christ as coming *incognito*. Christ, for Kierkegaard, is a divine being, and he also holds that between God and the human race there is 'an infinite qualitative difference'. So how could God be in Christ, or how could Jesus be the revelation of God, or how could Jesus Christ be the God-man? Kierkegaard's answer is that this is the supreme paradox, above reason. But given what he says about these matters, the paradox looks like a sheer impossibility. He does in fact tell us that the human historical Jesus is so far from being a revelation of the Christ of God that we learn nothing about the Christ from the historical manifestation in Jesus.

[F]rom history one can learning nothing about Christ. For if one learns little or much about Him [Jesus], or anything at all, He (who is thus known) is not He who in truth He is, i.e., one learns to know nothing about Him, or one learns to know something incorrect about Him, one is deceived. History makes Christ out to be another than He truly is, and so one learns to know a lot about ... Christ? No, not about Christ, for about Him nothing can be known, He can only be believed.[9]

I think there is considerable confusion in the paragraph just quoted. If we take it at what appears to be face-value, we are being asked to believe that Christ (the divine Logos) is *not* revealed in Jesus, that if we think we learn about the Christ from studying the human Jesus, we are mistaken, that the human historical Jesus is someone other than the Christ, that Christian theology can take only the form of the *via negativa* in the strictest sense, that we are required to believe in some one about whom we know nothing. All this seems to me to be in blatant contradiction to central convictions of the Christian faith. Perhaps it sometimes looked that way to Kierkegaard himself. So he writes elsewhere:

God did not assume the form of a servant to make a mockery of men; hence it cannot be his intention to pass through the world in such manner that no single human being becomes aware of his presence. He will therefore doubtless give some sort of sign.[10]

It may be doubted, however, whether Kierkegaard ever succeeded in extricating himself from some of the tangles into which he had strayed. Perhaps he would not have wanted to do so. But we find something else which is perhaps closer to what I was calling 'spiritual discernment' a little way back in our discussion. In his *Training in Christianity* – really an answer to the question, 'How does one become a Christian?' – Kierkegaard declares, 'Only through the consciousness of sin is there entrance to [Christianity], and the wish to enter in by any other way is the crime of *lèse-majesté*'.[11] Here, I think, we do have a transposition or shift of key from one mode of awareness to another, a shift from the historian's study of Jesus, a study which might well include an attempt to reconstruct his thinking and motivations, to a different mode of perception, namely, the spiritual impact of Jesus on the percipient. This is not just a feeling devoid of any cognitive content – it is a new self-awareness in relation to Jesus, indeed, produced by Jesus. It is not an empirical discovery about Jesus but a spiritual perception, in which Jesus is seen not just in his historic humanity but as the embodiment of the Logos, as the Christ. It is the kind of perception that Peter had when he recognized Jesus as the Christ, and was told, according to St Matthew, 'Flesh and blood has not revealed this to you' (Matt. 16.17), or, as we might say nowadays, this is no ordinary empirical recognition.

There are other important points that could be made about Kierkegaard's religious epistemology but these can be left for the present and it is time for us to pay attention to the other thinker in our comparison, John Henry Newman. Like Kierkegaard, Newman even in his early writings was working on problems of faith and reason and defending the autonomy of faith against the encroachments of those rationalists who claimed an omnicompetence for reason. Since Newman was about twelve years older than Kierkegaard, he began publishing nearly a decade earlier than the Danish writer, and it is interesting that already in 1835, in Tract 73, later republished with the title 'On the Introduction of Rationalistic Principles into Revealed Religion', Newman used precisely the same metaphor as Kierkegaard was to do later when he wrote of reason making a 'collision' with faith; for, he claimed, 'faith is in its very nature the acceptance of what our reason cannot reach'.[12]

Just as Kierkegaard recognized two possibilities when reason makes its collision, that is to say, either one has to make the leap of faith into a different medium or mode of thought, or one has to take offence and turn away, so Newman can visualize a situation where 'in the presence of faith, reason bows and retires', as well as situations in which reason has become an obstacle to faith. And just as Kierkegaard, while fully accepting the reality of revelation, was modest about expounding the revelation in theological formulae to the extent of earning the description 'negative theologian', so Newman had his famous 'principle of reserve'. This was not just an educational device, still less was it an attempt to deceive his readers or hearers. It was a recognition that truths that are spiritually discerned may not be amenable to being fully spelled out in words.

Although Newman uses a different vocabulary from Kierkegaard, there are profound similarities between them in their treatment of the relations of faith and reason. The reason to which both are opposed is not reason in the broad sense of the word, but an abstract or, if you like, impoverished reason which has been separated from the stream of personal life, a reason that has been reduced to mere 'syllogizing', to use one of Newman's words. The knowing or cognizing for which both of them are seeking to find a place belongs to the region of the fully personal. I wrote above that to understand Kierkegaard demands a certain 'empathy' on the part of the reader, because he is not dealing with abstract ideas, but drawing ideas from the context of personal life without separating them from that life. I was interested to find that Bernard Reardon uses this same word 'empathy' in writing about Newman. He says:

> Newman's writings – sermon, treatise, private letter, polemical pamphlet – not only instruct or exhort or amuse; they have the added power of the work of art to create *empathy*, to move the reader into the author's own frame of mind, to share his hopes and disappointments. The student of Newman's philosophy must therefore be prepared to approach it not only critically – for criticism has little difficulty in exposing its evasions and inconsistencies – but with personal understanding. *Cor ad cor loquitur.*[13]

Up to this point, I have been drawing attention to parallels between Newman and Kierkegaard. In general terms, both of them were concerned to limit the role of reason in matters of religion, for just as religion affects the whole human person, so its roots must be sought in the total personal experience. It cannot be adequately defended and still less can it be discredited by theoretical reasoning exercised in abstraction from the affective, moral and volitional life of the total personal being. But when we explore this position further, we find that there are quite important differences between Kierkegaard and Newman and we have to bring these into the open and, if possible, understand how they are to be explained.

I

A reading of the two authors may suggest that Kierkegaard is more antagonistic to reason than Newman. Both men, of course, underwent profound spiritual struggles, and had conversion experiences that shook them to the depths of their being, so we can understand that anything that might look like superficial syllogizing would not have much appeal to either of them. They had *known* in themselves (and I deliberately say 'known') something that seemed to them more firmly based than any argument. But in spite of this, both of them use arguments and defend theses when it suits their purpose to do so, and indeed if they had not done so, would we bother to read them? But a difference does emerge. Newman attaches importance to probability, and had been deeply influenced by Bishop Butler's saying that probability is the guide of life.[14] In the *Apologia*, Newman summarizes his view on probability thus:

> He who has made us has so willed that in mathematics indeed we arrive at certitude by rigorous demonstration, but in religious inquiry we arrive at certitude by accumulated probabilities – inasmuch as he who has willed that we should so act, co-operates with us in our acting, and thereby bestows on us certitude which rises higher than the logical force of our conclusions.[15]

In *A Grammar of Assent*, this teaching is spelled out more fully. First, there is the distinction between notional and real assent. 'In its notional assents, the mind contemplates its own creations instead of things, in real, it is directed toward things, represented by the impressions which they have left on the imagination.'[16] In the former case, we can recognize what we have been calling abstract reasoning, in the second the assent of the whole person. The distinction is known also to Kierkegaard, but where he differs is in disallowing the cumulative influence of probabilities. In Kierkegaard's view, the will has an important role in faith, therefore the lower the probability of something, the greater the effort of will required to believe it. Faith increases in direct ratio to the risk of being mistaken! 'For without risk, there is no faith; the more objective security, the less inwardness (for inwardness is precisely subjectivity), and the less objective security the more profound the possible inwardness.'[17] This seems to me a perverse argument. I find myself much more ready to go along with Newman who illustrates the power of cumulative probabilities by a train of thought that had often been used before his time:

> We know that a regular polygon, inscribed in a circle, its sides being continually diminished, tends to become that circle, as its limit; but it vanishes before it has coincided with the circle, so that its tendency to be the circle, though ever nearer fulfilment, never in fact gets beyond a tendency. In like manner, the conclusion in a real or concrete question is foreseen and predicted, rather than actually attained.[18]

Newman is careful to point out that there is always a gap between the point to which the cumulated probabilities have brought us and the conclusion to which they point, so that he is not denying that there must be a 'leap of faith', to use the Kierkegaardian expression, but the leap has been prepared. For instance, the traditional arguments for the existence of God may severally be unable to get beyond a greater or less measure of probability, but writers such as Basil Mitchell and Richard Swinburne have claimed that they do have a cumulative force. By comparison, Kierkegaard's leap seems to be an isolated and unsupported performance, and some people, myself included, would be perturbed by its seemingly arbitrary character.

But in fairness to Kierkegaard, it might be claimed that in leaving aside probabilities, he is making clear that the leap from facts to faith, so to speak, is not merely leaping beyond the evidence but is a leap into a different kind of discourse – *eis allo genos*, as he is fond of saying. But then the question arises whether there is any way of bridging the gap between the two types of discourse, and I doubt that either Newman or Kierkegaard has a convincing answer to that question.

Also, they may be closer than I have suggested. I have in mind what Newman says about the illative sense. He tells us, 'It is a rule to itself and appeals to no judgement beyond its own.'[19] It appears to be a kind of intuitive awareness that one has reached the truth, an awareness that brings with it its own certitude. This, I think, may be compared to Kierkegaard's remarks on truth. He distinguishes between objective truth, the kind that can be printed in books and is then available to anyone who reads the books, and subjective truth, which is known only through an inward experience in which it is made one's own, incorporated into one's being. This is the kind that St John's gospel seems to have in mind, when we read the words of Jesus, 'I am the way, the truth and the life' (John 14.6). Here the truth is inseparable from the way and the life. In a famous passage, Kierkegaard declares:

> Here is a definition of truth: the objective uncertainty held fast in the appropriation of the most passionate inwardness, is the truth, the highest truth there is for one who exists. There where the way swings off (and where that is cannot be said objectively, for that precisely is the subjectivity) objective knowledge is put in suspension. Objectively then he has only the uncertainty, but it is just this that intensified the infinite passion of his inwardness. And truth precisely is this venture, to choose the objectively uncertain with the passion of the infinite.[20]

Does this come close to Newman's idea of the illative sense? One possible difference is that whereas Newman was in search of certitude, Kierkegaard thought that faith is always precarious, as if one had been thrown into seventy thousand fathoms of water, to use one of his expressions.

II

Both Newman and Kierkegaard are seeking to break out of narrowly abstract rationalism, and both turn to the ethical sphere in order to broaden the basis for faith. But here again there is a significant difference. We have seen that Kierkegaard claims that it is the sense of sin that brings a human being towards the path of faith, an inward discontent that recognizes that one is falling short of what one is called to be. In Newman, it is not the negative phenomenon of sin but the positive phenomenon of conscience that performs this office. For Newman, conscience is indeed the voice of God. He believes, like the philosopher Kant, that morality has an absolute claim upon us, and a strong case can be made that this claim is indeed absolute, for if we go against conscience and flout the moral claim, surely we thereby destroy our own humanity and give up the claim to be truly human beings. Yet the recognition of the absoluteness of the moral demand is also tantamount to recognizing that here we have to do with a reality that transcends human reality, for nothing human has this kind of absolute quality. For Newman, conscience is the channel by which every human being may be addressed by God. Indeed, he goes even further and declares that 'conscience is the aboriginal Vicar of Christ'.[21]

I do not know how widely such views were held in Newman's time, but they are probably not very common today when morality, so far from being founded in any divine reality, has become to a large extent a matter of personal preference. As Alasdair MacIntyre has said, 'With the demise of the belief that man has an end and that moral laws derive from God, moral judgements lose any clear status, and the sentences which express them lose any undebatable meaning.'[22] I suspect that the state of affairs described by MacIntyre will eventually prove to be unstable and that we shall be eventually compelled to seek a firmer ground for the moral life, one closer to Newman's.

By finding the pointer to faith in conscience Newman seems to take a more affirmative path than Kierkegaard, who claimed that the sense of sin is the presupposition of faith. I say Newman is more affirmative at this point, for in emphasizing conscience, he is thinking along lines similar to those twentieth-century theologians (Rahner is the obvious example) who have claimed that the human being has the capacity for transcendence towards God.

There is, however, another difference between Newman and Kierkegaard, and this time it is Kierkegaard who has the advantage. In the treatise *Fear and Trembling*, Kierkegaard envisages a situation in which conscience is *not* the voice of God. Admittedly, his handling of the issue is controversial. But we are reminded that sometimes conscience is simply the voice of the culture or society to which we belong, and that in exceptional cases we may be called to obey God rather than men. Kierkegaard takes the difficult case of Abraham when he is commanded by God to sacrifice his son. This goes against morality, but is taken to be a higher command that results even in the suspension of the ethical. If one accepts Kierkegaard's analysis, then one has also to recognize that conscience may be mistaken. Indeed, it is difficult to see how there could ever be moral progress unless sometimes an individual did not experience a conflict between conscience and what he believed to be a higher principle.

III

This brings us to a further divergence between Kierkegaard and Newman. Kierkegaard is very much the individualist, Newman is a man of the church, the community. Both men, of course, were highly complex characters, and one could find individualistic traits in Newman as well as Kierkegaard. Both were celibates, and both were distinctive and independent in their ideas.

But their attitudes to the past were very different. Newman had a romantic respect for antiquity and idealized it. We have already seen that Kierkegaard was dismissive of history. It is likely that this had something to do with their very different understandings of the church. For Kierkegaard, the individual's spiritual experience was of supreme importance, and increasingly he saw the church as an obstacle which robbed believers of a genuine relation to Christ. If romanticism means, among other things, attaching importance to the emotions, then Kierkegaard's romanticism is to be seen not in an idealizing of historic Christendom but in the solitary mood of anxiety, which is the mood that leads to the consciousness of sin, which in turn is the awareness that prepares for the reception of revelation.

So whereas Newman, with his sense of the historic church, was deeply moved by Augustine's words, *Securus judicat orbis terrarum*, and reckoned the influence of these words to have been an important factor in bringing about his conversion, one suspects that the words would have made little or no impression on Kierkegaard. Again, whereas Newman eventually came to accept the need for an infallible *historical* authority in matters of faith, one may suppose that, in spite of his progressive disillusionment with Luther and the Lutheran church, Kierkegaard's individualism would have prevented him from ever becoming a Roman Catholic.

I do not know whether we can agree with Reardon's judgement, quoted earlier, that Newman and Kierkegaard are the two outstanding religious figures of the nineteenth century. Certainly, in an age of increasing materialism and secularism, they did much to vindicate and invigorate the spiritual nature of human beings. They followed original and remarkably parallel paths, but they also diverged at various points. If they left us with insights that are still worth exploring, they left also unanswered questions that we must take up anew in our time.

Notes

1. Bernard M. G. Reardon, *From Coleridge to Gore* (Longman 1971), p. 127.
2. Immanuel Kant, *Critique of Pure Reason* (Macmillan 1929), p. 29.
3. F. D. E. Schleiermacher, *The Christian Faith* (T. & T. Clark 1928), p. 12.
4. *Ibid.*, pp. 133–4.
5. S. Kierkegaard, *Philosophical Fragments* (Princeton U.P. 1936), p. 29.
6. *Ibid.*, p. 35.
7. D. R. Law, *Kierkegaard as Negative Theologian* (Oxford U.P. 1993), p. 82.
8. Kierkegaard, *Philosophical Fragments*, p. 87.
9. Kierkegaard, *Training in Christianity* (Princeton U.P. 1944), p. 28.
10. Kierkegaard, *Philosophical Fragments*, p. 44.
11. Kierkegaard, *Training in Christianity*, p. 71.
12. J. H. Newman, Tract 73, in Ian Ker, ed., *Newman the Theologian* (Collins 1990), p. 75.
13. Reardon, *op. cit.*, p. 129.
14. Joseph Butler, *Works* (O.U.P. 1896), I, p. 5.
15. Newman, *Apologia pro vita sua* (Sheed & Ward 1979), p. 134.
16. Newman, *A Grammar of Assent* (University of Notre Dame Press 1979), p. 76.
17. Kierkegaard, *Concluding Unscientific Postscript* (O.U.P. 1945), p. 188.
18. Newman, *Assent*, pp. 253–4.
19. *Ibid.*, p. 283.
20. Kierkegaard, *Postscript*, p. 182.
21. See Reardon, *op. cit.*, p. 140.
22. A. MacIntyre, *After Virtue* (University of Notre Dame Press 1984), p. 60.

6

Newman and Wittgenstein on the Rationality of Religious Belief

Cyril Barrett, SJ

Until comparatively recently, and even today, it may be considered eccentric to regard Newman as a philosopher, and preposterous to compare him with Wittgenstein. Yet Wittgenstein not only read Newman but admired him, though he did not agree with him. I have this on the authority of Yorick Smythies, an ex-student of his, and O. K. Bousma, another ex-student, also testifies to this.[1] But the best testimony comes from Wittgenstein himself in the first entry in *On Certainty* which reads: '(a curious [*komische*] remark of H. Newman)'.[2] Since the appearance of that book in 1969 quite a number of papers on Newman as a philosopher, many of them comparing him with Wittgenstein, have appeared. Here I shall draw on these comparisons and add considerably more of my own.

But first I shall pose a problem that faces both Newman and Wittgenstein, that of possible circularity in their method. Wittgenstein raises it with regard to Newman. According to Smythies, he once commented that in *The Grammar of Assent* Newman thought he was building his religious beliefs on a firm foundation of other beliefs, but in fact they were floating on air suspended from his faith. Basil Mitchell argues that the same can be said about Wittgenstein's own language games and forms of life. I shall discuss these claims later.

That it has taken so long to recognize Newman as a philosopher is not surprising, and for at least two reasons. In the first place, his knowledge of and interest in philosophy was limited. His chief preoccupation was with theology, apologetics and matters spiritual and pastoral. Apart from Locke, a little of Hume and

Mill's *Logic*, he knew hardly any modern philosophy, and seems to have been totally ignorant of German or other Continental philosophy. He regarded metaphysical proof as rare, immaterial and difficult to embrace. Nor was he sympathetic to the scientific model of the acquisition of truth which was currently regarded as the paradigm. Certainly, he would have nothing to do with it as a model for explaining religious belief. The view favoured by some apologists shaken by Darwinism and other scientific 'threats' to religious belief that religious belief was as scientifically grounded as history, textual criticism, archaeology and other disciplines that follow the scientific model was totally alien to his thought. On the other hand, he believed that a rational account of religious belief could be given, though not a scientific account. In that he differed from Kantians such as Schleiermacher who regarded religious belief as the product of feeling and intuition, rather than of thought or reasoning.

It was in his rational account of religious belief that he made his contribution to the philosophy of religion. Ironically, there were others thinking along similar lines on the Continent. The basic similarity between Newman and the Continentals was that they proposed an alternative to the natural sciences which they called spiritual science (*Geisteswissenschaft*). The seeds of this notion had been sown by Johann Gustav Droysen as early as 1857/8 in his *Historik* where he sketched out a methodology of historical research and made a distinction between *Erklärung* (explanation), which is the domain of the natural or exact sciences, and *Verstehen* (understanding) which is the domain of historical studies. This, strange to say, is an advance on Aristotle's account of science. For him, science not only described what is the case – that a cow has two stomachs *and* chews the cud – but that this *must be* the case, i.e. it is because a cow *must* regurgitate barely digestible grass that it *must* have two stomachs – and this explains why what is the case *must be so*. This is not possible in history, unless you are a determinist, which neither Newman nor Wittgenstein was. So the best that history – and, by extension, ethics, aesthetics, metaphysics, religious knowledge, and suchlike disciplines – can do is to help us to *understand* why what is the case is the case. But it was not until 1883 with Wilhelm Dilthey's seminal work, *Einleitung in die Geisteswissenschaften* (*Introduction to the Sciences of the Spirit*) that the notion was extended beyond history to ethics and religious belief. Over a decade earlier, in 1870, Newman had published his *An Essay in Aid of a Grammar of Assent*.

It is interesting that he gave his work the title 'grammar'. To claim that Wittgenstein derived his notion of philosophical grammar from Newman would possibly be going too far, but the ideas are very similar. What were more similar were Newman's distinctions between formal and informal reasoning or inference, and between real and notional assent. For Newman, as for Wittgenstein, formal reason was logical reason, such as is (or should be) used in philosophical arguments and scientific discussions. It is basically syllogistic, if not mathematically formal. Informal reasoning is what Newman called 'cumulative reasoning' – that is, a lot of reasons are piled up together with no necessary logical connection, but are persuasive by their cumulative force, as in a judicial argument or a discussion about morality or history or religious belief.

The distinction between notional and real assent turns on the question of commitment. Someone who gives notional assent commits himself only to accepting the truth of the assertion, even if that truth has practical consequences. Newman gives various instances: the evil and absurdity of duelling and of slavery, the necessity of maintaining an efficient defence force, and so on. People gave notional assent to these propositions, paid lip-service to them, but neither did anything about them or intended to do anything, until someone like Wilberforce, in the case of slavery, gave a real, practical, active assent to them, and turned the notion into reality. In the *Grammar of Assent* Newman introduces a lengthy quotation from a piece he had written thirty years earlier in criticism of Lord Brougham's and Sir Robert Peel's suggestion that religious belief should be given a scientific basis. His argument can be summarized by this passage:

> First comes knowledge, then a view, then reasoning, and then belief. This is why science has so little of a religious tendency; deductions have no power of persuasion. The heart is commonly reached, not through reason, but through the imagination, by means of direct impressions, by the testimony of facts and events, by history, by descriptions. Persons influence us, voices melt us, ... deeds inflame us.[3]

How Wittgenstein must have taken pleasure in that passage!

Wittgenstein had abandoned Catholicism at the age of sixteen, largely from reading Schopenhauer under the influence of his bluestocking sister, Gretl. But during the disastrous Carpatian campaign of June 1916, his views changed. On 11 June 1916, he

wrote in his notebook: 'What do I know about God and the purpose of life?'[4] And on 8 July he lists what be believes about God.
Again, on 2 August an entry reads: 'Yes, my work has broadened
from the foundations of logic to the essence of the world' (*NB*, p.
79). It is clear that his thinking had completely changed. His
interest in the philosophy of logic was now related to his inner,
spiritual life. More than that, the philosophical logic took on
another role. It became a contrast with what Wittgenstein regarded as the ordinary use of language and what cannot be said in
ordinary language and yet is the only thing worth talking about.
Though these last remarks take up only three pages of the final
version of the *Tractatus* perhaps that was too much.

It may not seem immediately evident that Wittgenstein's
distinction between what can and cannot be said in ordinary
language and Newman's distinction between deductive and
cumulative reasoning have much in common, but they have. In
Wittgenstein's terminology what we can say in ordinary language
are *statements of fact*, of what is the case, what *happens to be so*.
Some of these statements may be reports of observation, others
are logical deductions, and scientific. What cannot be said,
according to Wittgenstein, are expressions of value, religious, ethical, aesthetical, etc. But this does not mean you cannot speak
about them. It only means that your speech will be circuitous,
and this sounds very like Newman's cumulative reasoning and the
hermeneutics' *Verstehen*.

There is also an element of neo-Kantianism, another feature of
hermeneutics, in Wittgenstein's attitude to ethical, aesthetic and,
presumably, religious values. They are transcendental. That is,
they cannot be put into propositional form. 'It is impossible for
there to be propositions of ethics', he says; 'ethics cannot be put
into words'.[5] This does not mean that we cannot speak about
them, only that what we say is not like saying grass is green and
ravens are black. To say 'it is wrong to kill an innocent person deliberately' is not to state a fact about the world that happens to be
the case. But, in Wittgenstein's view, and I have no doubt that it
would be Newman's also, this is no hardship. Statements of fact
count for very little in Wittgenstein's book. He says: 'We feel that
even when all *possible* scientific questions have been answered, the
problems of life remain completely untouched' (*TLP*, 6.52). And
this may throw some light on the famous last sentence of the
Tractatus: 'What we cannot speak about we must pass over in
silence.'

Bertrand Russell, to his credit, in his preface to the *Tractatus* recognized that the last few pages, which he did not accept (and possibly did not understand), were possibly those on which Wittgenstein would want to lay most stress. Most readers, however, were baffled by those last few pages and ignored them as irrelevant. The Logical Positivists, on the other hand, greeted them, particularly the last three entries, triumphantly as driving the last nail into the coffin of metaphysics which Kant had built. F. P. Ramsey added that not only do we have to pass over that of which we cannot speak but we cannot whistle it either, thus reducing it to banality by taking it literally.[6] Literally it is trite. Of course we must pass over in silence that of which we cannot speak. What else can we do? This should have alerted the Logical Positivists to the possibility that that last sentence did not mean quite what it appeared to mean, and, thus, spared them the shock they got later in the decade when they discovererd that Wittgenstein was not a Logical Positivist after all.

It would be an exaggeration to suggest that Newman's and Wittgenstein's positions on science and religious belief were close. Wittgenstein was approaching the question from the point of view of language, of what can and cannot be said; Newman was approaching it from the more strictly epistemological point of types of reasoning and types of assent. Newman would probably be horrified to learn that what he arrived at by informal inference, namely, a religious belief, cannot be put into words and must be passed over in silence. But he might be heartened to learn that this does not mean that he must remain dumb. All it means is that he should not try to put it into the linguistic mould of scientific propositions. With this he would have wholeheartedly agreed, since this was the whole thrust of his *Grammar of Assent.*

There we must leave the early Wittgenstein. When we come to the later, the resemblances to Newman's way of thinking become much closer. One of the major insights of his later period was that language is not a detached and abstract thing as treated by logicians and linguists, laid down on a laboratory slab like a lifeless specimen. Language is a living thing. It gets its life from the use to which it is put in living situations and the purposes for which it is used. Wittgenstein in *Philosophical Investigations* described language in terms of 'forms of life' and 'language games'. This is closer to Newman's informal inference and real assent. It is down to earth. It does not mean that logic, mathematics, and science cannot be language games and forms of life. They are. But what is of interest is that other disciplines and forms of discourse are too. And if they happen to be religious or ethical, aesthetical or legal, political, or just generally social or cultural, they are no less language games dependent on particular forms of life. In other words, they are not to be dismissed simply because they are not scientific. But – much more importantly – they must not be understood or judged by so-called scientific criteria but on their own terms, according to the rules of their own language game and in relation to their own form of life.

I should be deeply surprised if Newman would not have welcomed this notion of forms of life. It fits neatly, even if not expressed in the same terms, with his assumptions, presuppositions, traditional ways of thinking and living. This is borne out in Wittgenstein's remarks on ethics and religion, published under the apposite title, *Culture and Value*,[7] but even more fully in his three lectures on religious belief, delivered in 1939, recorded by Alan Rush Rhees and published in *Lectures and Conversations*.[8]

Perhaps the most pertinent comparison with which to start is to be found in what Wittgenstein says about the rationality of religious belief. He says that religious belief is not reasonable in the ordinary sense: 'Reasons look entirely different from normal reasons. They are, in a way, quite inconclusive. The point is that if there were evidence, this in fact would destroy the whole business' (*LC*, p. 56). This echoes, if unconsciously, Newman's distinction between informal inference or cumulative reasoning and deductive inference or formal reasoning (Wittgenstein's 'normal reasons'). Even more pertinent is a remark which succinctly summarizes Newman's thinking on reasoning in support of religious belief: 'As it were, the belief as formulated on the evidence can only be a last resort – in which a number of ways of thinking and acting crystallize and come together' (*LC*, p. 56).

There are two points to be made here. Firstly, that a number of ways of thinking and acting come together and crystallize seems to be just what Newman is saying about cumulative argument and the kinds of reasons it brings together. Secondly, it is a last resort. That again is in accord with Newman's thinking. He did not think that the ordinary believer came to his beliefs by cumulative reasoning, only that the beliefs were not unreasonable, as can be shown by informal inference. But perhaps the most striking coincidence of thought is their view of the role of evidence. Newman says in *The Via Media of the Anglican Church* with reference to notional as opposed to real assent: 'When we are not personally concerned, even the highest evidence does not move us; when we are concerned, the very slightest is enough.'⁹ And here is Wittgenstein:

> he has what you might call an unshakeable belief. It will show, not by reasoning or by appeal to ordinary grounds for belief, but rather by regulating for in [*sic*] all his life ... This [in] one sense must be called the firmest of all beliefs, because the man risks things on account of it which he would not do on things which are by far better established for him. Although he distinguishes between things well-established and not well-established. (*LC,* p. 54)

This leads to yet another coincidence of thought. In that passage from *The Via Media* from which I have just quoted we read: 'Action is the criterion of true faith, as determining accurately whether we connect the thought of God with the thought of ourselves, whether we love Him, or regard Him otherwise than we regard the existence of the solar system.'¹⁰

This has clearly to do with notional and real assent. But it has also to do with a criterion of true belief. This was precisely the question Wittgenstein was asking just before the passage I quoted. Speaking of belief in the Last Judgement, he asks: 'how are we to know whether to say he believes this will happen, or not? Asking him is not enough. He will probably say he has proof.' But the real criterion is how he regulates his life. Does he take the belief seriously? Does he prepare himself for the Lord's coming or, to vary Newman's analogy, regard it with no more interest than an eclipse of the sun? Here Newman and Wittgenstein seem once again to be speaking with one voice even if the wording is somewhat different.

Wittgenstein went far beyond Newman in differentiating formal or deductive inference and notional assent from informal inference and real assent. He will have nothing to do with probabilities, possibilities, opinions or hypotheses. For him it would be absurd to talk about the possibility or probability of there being a Judgement Day as though it were a future event like another Ice Age. As he says:

> Suppose, for instance, we knew people who ... make forecasts for years and years ahead; and they described some sort of a Judgement Day. Queerly enough, even if there were such a thing, and even if it were more convincing than I have described, belief in this happening won't be at all a religious belief. (*LC,* p. 56)

Although much more can be gleaned from Wittgenstein's lectures on religious belief, I must pass now to the much richer source from which to garner similarities of thought between Newman and Wittgenstein. I refer, of course, to Wittgenstein's last work, *On Certainty*. Here I can do nothing more than outline the main resemblances.

Both Newman and Wittgenstein were beset by the spectre of scepticism. Newman records of his youth (taken from a youthful account): 'I though life might be a dream, or I an Angel, and all this world a deception, my fellow-angels by a playful device concealing themselves from me, and deceiving me with the semblance of a material world.'[11] His scepticism was fuelled by reading Locke and Hume, though, strangely, Berkeley did not have such a profoundly adverse effect, possibly because Newman was a Berkeleyian already. However, by the time he came to write the *Grammar of Assent* he had rejected the Lockian and Humean solutions to the problem that lies in wait for all empirical sceptics, namely, the need to accept some empirical propositions as certain in order to doubt others. Moreover, the fact that, unlike tautologies, all empirical propositions are open to being doubted and none are indubitable, does not mean that they can be doubted at will peradventure. Both Locke and Hume recognized this. Locke feebly attributed it to ordinary common sense. Hume, only a little less feebly, attributed it to natural human instinct, as if that explained anything. At least Newman held to the belief that there is a rational solution to this problem, and, if G. E. Moore and Wittgenstein are correct, he was at least moving in the right direction.

To be more precise: seriously to doubt a proposition is implicitly to assume that there is a way of proving it true or false, otherwise one has to say that it is just meaningless. Moreover, one cannot just say 'I doubt it' or 'I don't believe you'. There is an onus on the speaker to show grounds for doubt, not just on the believer to support his belief. Now, if the reason for believing an empirical proposition, such that I am talking to you (whether or not you are listening to me or can even hear me) is such that a belief to the contrary is too absurd, then it is reasonable to entertain that belief. It is no less reasonable to build an argument based on this and other such beliefs. How high this edifice of reasonable beliefs can be built is a moot point, and I shall return to it. Newman lists a number of empirical propositions that he regards as being immune from reasonable doubt even though they cannot be proved. Newman's list almost exceeds Moore's: that I exist; that I shall die some day; that Great Britain is an island; and so on. Unlike Moore, he did not use them in defence of common sense against unreasonable scepticism, but as part of the building material of his cumulative argument.

Wittgenstein had another use for them, and invented a new concept, that of the 'hinge [*Angel*] proposition', best explained by himself:

> We know with the same certainty with which we believe *any* mathematical proposition how the letters A and B are pronounced, what the colour of human blood is called [etc.]
>
> That is to say, the *questions* that we raise and our *doubts* depend on the fact that some propositions are exempt from doubt, and are as it were like hinges on which those turn.
>
> ... it belongs to the logic of our scientific investigations that certain things are *in fact* not doubted.
>
> ... We just can't investigate everything, and for that reason we are forced to rest content with assumption. If I want the door to turn, the hinges must stay put. (*OC*, pp. 43–4, 340–3)

I think Newman might have been pleased with this and with much else in *On Certainty* where echoes of his problems and his thought keep cropping up.

Finally, to that quip of Wittgenstein's with which we started. Wittgenstein accuses Newman, at least implicitly, of circularity, of assuming what he is attempting to justify. Many of the considerations invoked in support of assent to Christian belief are themselves Christian beliefs or interpretations within the Christian tradition, so, in effect, Christian belief supports itself, which is precisely what Wittgenstein's imagery is designed to convey. Moreover, two can play that game. If Newman can justify the rationality of religious beliefs by his cumulative method, why can't a Muslim or an atheist do the same? How, then, are we to adjudicate between religious beliefs? Mitchell believes that Wittgenstein himself was faced with the same problem in relation to forms of life.[12]

Newman was not unaware of this last difficulty, and states it most clearly in one of his *University Sermons*. And he would agree, as would Wittgenstein, that there is no independent standard of rationality by which this matter can be resolved. Newman puts it like this: 'When men understand each other's meaning, they see, for the most part, that controversy is either superfluous or hopeless'[13] and Wittgenstein like this: 'Well, suppose I say Christian

ethics is the right one. Then I am making a judgment of value. It
amounts to *adopting* Christian ethics. It is not like saying that one
of these physical theories must be the right one.'[14]

But would Newman have allowed that the Muslim or the atheist is rational in his beliefs? I am not in a position to say what
Newman would have said if the question had been put to him.
There is nothing to suggest that it would contradict his argument
if he did allow that. What he was arguing was that Christian belief is rational. For this argument to hold it is not necessary to
prove that every other belief is irrational. Perhaps some are, if they
are self-contradictory or contradict obvious sense. But all need
not be irrational for Christianity to be rational. Newman's whole
point is that this is not formal reasoning of the A or not-A type.
That the Muslim or atheist may give a rational account of his
belief is not incompatible with the Christian giving a rational
account of his. This was undoubtedly Wittgenstein's view, since
he states explicitly in his lectures that even though he did not
share a religious belief, he would not call it unreasonable.

Finally, we come to the question of circularity. Most, if not all,
philosophers commenting on Newman believe that his argument
is circular. That seems to be unavoidable whatever allowances are
made. Even if one concedes that a set of neutral probabilities with
Christian interpretations could build up a rational case, which, if
not logically conclusive, justified (as it demanded) assent, this still
would not evade the criticism that the Christian interpretation
was based on faith and belief, and not on reason. So, ultimately,
belief is based on belief, which is circular.

However, if we were to say that Newman was misguided in
thinking that he was even informally *reasoning* the case for
Christian belief in particular, and religious belief in general, there
might be a better way of describing what he was doing. This
would be to say that what he was giving was not a piece of informal and cumulative reasoning in support of religious belief so
much as a *rational account* of the basis of Christian belief: why
Christians believe what they do and what that implies. In other
words, if the *Grammar of Assent* is seen as a rational exposé of
what Christian belief implies and involves, and not as a cumulative argument, there can be no question of circularity, since
nothing is being proved, even informally.

A parallel that might be taken is St Anselm's so-called ontolo-
gical argument. What makes it look like an argument (or rather,
arguments) is that he dragged in the fool who said in his heart

'there is no God'. This made it look like a refutation, whereas Anselm was speaking to his fellow monks, all of whom believed in God, and, had they not, would have been unimpressed by his arguments (as would the fool). What Anselm was in effect proving was that believing in God involved belief in a necessary, all-perfect, eternal being, and that that made sense. Implied in that account is its rationality. This is precisely what Wittgenstein had in mind when he wrote 'I think that what *believers* who have furnished such proofs have wanted to do is give their "belief" an intellectual analysis and foundation, although they themselves would never have come to believe as a result of such proofs' (*CV*, p. 85).

This would dispose of the belief-supporting-the-reason object-ion. But it is not exactly reason-supporting-belief either. To say that all that is involved in the *Grammar of Assent* is some kind of rational analysis of belief, and that this constitutes the rationality of religious belief, does not seem to do justice to Newman. But, at least, it gives us a different image. It is no longer reason sus-pended from the faith it is supposed to be supporting; it is faith supporting reason, and reason, thus supported, supporting faith. If you find this image hard to visualize, may I suggest that, when you next visit Dublin, you have a look at a bank in Dame Street. Its walls do not support the roof but are suspended from it. (Where else would you expect to find such a building?)

Notes

1. O. K. Bousma, *Wittgenstein: Conversations 1949–1951*, ed. J. L. Craft and R. E. Hustwit, New York, 1986.
2. Ludwig Wittgenstein, *On Certainty* (hereafter referred to as *OC*), Oxford, 1969, p. 2.
3. J. H. Newman, *An Essay in aid of a Grammar of Assent*, London, 1930, p. 92.
4. Ludwig Wittgenstein, *Notebooks 1914–1916* (hereafter referred to as *NB*), Oxford, 1961, p. 72.
5. Ludwig Wittgenstein, *Tractatus Logico-Philosophicus* (hereafter referred to as *TLP*), London, 1961, 6.42, 6.421.
6. F. P. Ramsay, *Foundations of Mathematics and Other Essays*, London, 1931, p. 238.
7. Ludwig Wittgenstein, *Culture and Value* (hereafter referred to as *CV*), Oxford, 1980.
8. Ludwig Wittgenstein, *Lectures and Conversations on Aesthetics. Psychology and Religious Belief*, edited by Cyril Barrett from students' notes of Wittgenstein's lectures (hereafter referred to as *LC*), Oxford, 1966.
9. J. H. Newman, *The Via Media of the Anglican Church*, London, 1877, vol. I, p. 86.
10. *Ibid.*, p. 87.
11. J. H. Newman, *Apologia pro vita sua*, ed. Martin J. Svaglic, Oxford, 1967, p. 16.
12. Basil Mitchell, 'Newman as a Philosopher', *Newman After a Hundred Years*, Oxford, 1990, ed. Ian Ker and Alan G. Hill, pp. 239–40.
13. J. H. Newman, *Oxford University Sermons*, London, 1872, p. 201.
14. Ludwig Wittgenstein, in *Philosophical Review*, 1966, p. 24.

7

Littlemore from Lucerne: Newman's Essay on Development *in Balthasarian Perspective*

Aidan Nichols, OP

It is not difficult to imagine Lucerne viewed from Littlemore. The discovery of the Alps by Englishmen was a part of that Romantic Movement some of whose garments the Oxford divines stole for the better setting forth of the Gospel. Not only the miscreant Shelley and Byron but also the Wordsworths, William and Dorothy, left prose and poetry worthy of inclusion in any Alpine anthology. In 1829 Walter Scott published his 'Swiss' novel, *Anne of Geierstein*. In 1835 John Ruskin made his first visit to Switzerland at the age of sixteen. Standing on the Col de la Faucille, 'the spectacle opened to me the Holy Land of my future work, and my true home in this world'.[1] J. M. W. Turner, Ruskin's *beau idéal* of the visual artist, had made his first visit as long ago as 1804 and would continue to travel and sketch there until 1844; his *The Lake of Thun* was perhaps his last water-colour and final canvas before his death in 1851.[2] In 1845 Dickens was at Lucerne and would return the following year to write *Dombey and Son* at Lausanne; in 1848 Matthew Arnold could be found at Thun or in the Oberland; in 1849 George Eliot was at Geneva and Elizabeth Barrett Browning at Interlaken, by now almost an English colony. In the course of the 1850s Ruskin poured out the volumes of his *Modern Painters: Their Superiority in the Art of Landscape Painting to all the Ancient Masters*; in an epilogue he would re-affirm the connection between the mountains and his aesthetic *credo*, with its central claim that

> the knowledge of what is beautiful leads on, and is the first step,

to the knowledge of the things which are lovely and of good report; and [that] the laws, the life, and the joy of beauty in the material world of God are as eternal and sacred parts of his creation
as, in the world of spirits, virtue; and in the world of angels,
praise.[3]

By that decade, English travellers could plan their journey with
the help of a variety of guide-books, from Daniel Wall's *The
Traveller's Guide through Switzerland*, written as early as 1819, to
John Murray's *A Handbook for Travellers in Switzerland*, published
in 1838. Most visitors now wished to go higher, in plain contra-
diction of that pre-Romantic sensibility which made Bishop
Berkeley, crossing Mont Cenis in 1714, a disagreeable companion,
put 'out of humour by the most horrible precipices', or John
Spence in 1730 declare without a trace of irony, 'I should like the
Alps very much if it were not for the hills'.[4] They could select
among Alfred Wills' *Wanderings in the High Alps* (1856), T. W.
Hinchliff's *Summer Months among the Alps* (1857), and *Peaks,
Passes and Glaciers* (1859), edited by the first president of the
Alpine Club, John Ball. In 1863, Thomas Cook organized his first
tour to Switzerland. Entering the country at Geneva, the Cook's
tourist crossed Canton Vaud to the Valais, did full justice to the
Bernese Oberland, and proceeded via the Lake of Brienz to
Lucerne where the ascent of the Rigi formed the climax of the trip
prior to leaving Switzerland for France again via Neuchâtel.[5] The
beginnings of mass tourism (the 21-day holiday cost, inclusively,
£19 17s 6d) did little to deter the English literary class. In 1864
Mrs Gaskell was at Pontresina writing *Mothers and Daughters*, in
1865 Christina Rossetti almost everywhere, and in 1866 two celebrated Englishmen reached Lucerne. One was Sir George Grove,
the creator of the great encyclopaedia of music; the other was
John Henry Newman.

It cannot be said that Newman covered himself with glory
precisely as a student of Swiss scenery. Whereas in the Suisse
Romande the weather had been bad, in the Oberland and at
Lucerne it was, he admitted, excellent. Nonetheless, the comments in his letters on the ambient beauty of landscape are per-
functory. He reserved more space for querulousness about
personal comfort – the beds at once too comfortable (the upper
mattress) and not comfortable enough (the lower), the food disagreeable – too varied, though he took in his stride the serving of
a seagull. Newman could no doubt have met numerous Oxford-
trained clergymen: over sixty places of worship of the Church of

England had been or were being built, while muscular Kingsleyan parsons were two-a-penny on the mountain ascents. Not unreasonably, he was more preoccupied with staying within the Catholic regions of a chequered eiderdown of a country: he wanted the opportunity to say or attend mass daily. The historic significance of his Swiss journey lies in the fact that it was then, as he revealed to Aubrey de Vere in a letter of 1870, that the key notion of the *Grammar of Assent* came to him,[6] and that central notion – that certitude is itself a form of assent – he 'pursued ... about the Lake of Lucerne', where hopefully things had improved since Wall had noted that 'the navigation is not dangerous, provided the steersman and rowers be not intoxicated'.[7] Perhaps it was as well he had not postponed his visit till after Queen Victoria's two years later, when the Lake would become quite distractingly bedizened by strings of hotels and tearooms re-named or entitled for the first time in her honour.

Knowing no German, Newman may be forgiven his failure to realize that Lucerne was the theological centre of Swiss Catholicism, and his ignorance that in 1827, when as a tutor at Oriel his own short-lasting theological liberalism had reached its zenith (or nadir), there had died in the lake-city one Joseph Heinrich Alois Gügler, a figure of seminal importance for the Germanophone Catholic theology of the nineteenth and twentieth centuries,[8] the star of the *Luzerner Schule* which discovered the theological possibilities of European Romanticism a generation before its equivalent at Tübingen,[9] a profound influence on Möhler whose notions of the correlative development of Church and doctrine gave Newman himself confidence that his own *Essay on Development* might not be un-Catholic, and, above all, among the principal spurs – perhaps indeed the *chief* stimulus – to the theological aesthetics of his fellow-townsman Hans Urs von Balthasar whose work constitutes among other things a superb dogmatic expansion and re-thinking of the thesis Newman put forward in tentative historical and apologetic guise in 1845.[10]

My main aim here is, then, to look at Littlemore from Lucerne, that is, to draw out of the corpus left by the most distinguished modern Swiss theologian, Balthasar, highlights that will illuminate that key work of the most distinguished English theologian of modern times, Newman.

Balthasar never singled out Newman as one of the many writers, from the Fathers to contemporary poets and dramatists, whom he

honoured with a monograph or a distinct essay – all by way of ex-
hibiting the resources of theological tradition as well as re-taking
possession of those resources for his own distinctive purposes.
This has obscured two important facts, and these are, first, the
key role played in Balthasar's corpus at large by references to
Newman and Newmanian ideas, and secondly, the way Balthasar's
score provides richer dogmatic orchestration for a number of
Newmanian themes relevant not least to the 1845 *Essay*.

Let me offer an overview of the allusions to, or expositions of
Newman's ideas in the great trilogy – *Herrlichkeit*, the theological
aesthetics, *Theodramatik*, the theological dramatics, and
Theologik, the theological logic, before concentrating more especially on what Balthasar can add to a dogmatic understanding
of Newman's idea of development as laid out most fully, but by
no means exclusively, in that treatise of the year of his conversion
to Rome.

Balthasar regarded Newman's conversion as a major example of
what he termed the 'Pauline' element in the total structure of ecclesial experience. Drawing on the paradigm case of the conversion of Saul of Tarsus, Balthasar proposed that an enduring factor
in the construction of distinctively Christian experience in the
Church lies in the phenomenon of what he called the 'ever-new
vertical irruption of new charisms which suddenly visit and fruc-
tify' her life.[11] The conversion to the Church, or to a more fully
ecclesial life, of certain individuals outstanding in their gifts of
nature and grace, can render the Church spiritually fruitful in
fresh ways. For Balthasar there are no charisms – that is, no
special gifts of the Spirit for the sanctification of individuals –
without concomitant calls to mission, without, namely, some
repercussion in a reorientation of life and consciousness in the
corporate existence of the Church, at any rate in given times and
places. Elsewhere, in the soon-to-be translated *Theologik*, when
speaking of the Spirit and the Church as factors in theological
logic, Balthasar contrasts the ecclesiastical hierarchy, whose chief
gift is the discernment of spirits, with the charismatic element
proper which can be moved to introduce some novelty whose
legitimacy may not at first sight be obvious to the Church of office – as with the innovatory understanding of Religious life represented in the sixteenth century not only by the founder of the
Society of Jesus but also by that pioneer of sisterhoods dedicated
to teaching, better known in the German-speaking lands than in
her own country, Mary Ward. Such Spirit-willed innovations

come normally, Balthasar comments, either from non-ordained believers or from 'priests enflamed by the Holy Ghost' – and it is in this last exalted category that Balthasar places the contribution of Newman.[12]

But in what, on Balthasar's view, scattered as this is through a medley of references in the trilogy, *did* Newman's specific contribution consist? The question can be answered by synthesizing those references. What Balthasar emphasizes about Newman is in the first place his experiential, cordial ('of the heart'), and holistic approach to the Gospel of Christ. Balthasar claims Newman as an outstanding witness for the defence in his own case for the vindication of believing experience – the ordinary spiritual experience of Christians, distinct from though intimately connected with mystical experience properly so called – as something internal to, and even decisive for, the theological enterprise. Though Balthasar is careful to construct his concept of Christian experience in such a way that it can never be *counterposed to* Church tradition or teaching whereas it can and does *amplify* both, he treats that experience nonetheless as the entrance of the believing person into those realities of which faith speaks. He sees Newman as a climactic representative of (in a term borrowed from Henri Bremond) that 'metaphysics of the saints' which, emphasizing the Christian life rather than speculation, renounced the idea of relationship with God as mediated via the cosmos because its own religious sensibility was animated throughout by the desire for an immediate (if Christ-centred) contact with God.[13] Locating Newman in this way with the Rhineland mystics, Loyola and the French school culminating in his fellow-Oratorian Pierre de Bérulle, would certainly help to explain his lack of responsiveness to the Alpine glories of his 1866 travels: Newman, we might say, preserved the distinctive emotional range of early nineteenth-century Romanticism, from awe to tenderness, but displaced from its customary stimuli in the experience of physical nature.

But then, after this praise of experiential holism, when Balthasar calls such a spiritual approach the emergence of a distinctive if incomplete Christian *metaphysics* we realize that he is not praising Newman's concern with experience for any anti-intellectual bias. Linking Newman to Pascal and Kierkegaard, he describes all three as speaking not only existentially but also objectively – *sachlich* – because 'they ... stood under Christ's fiery glance [the reference is surely to the opening vision of the

Johannine Apocalypse] which forbade them to engage in any digressive rhetoric and simply charged them to stand firm'.[14]

As Balthasar explains, with Newman the heart is the *foundation* of the intellect (as of the other particular faculties) – *not* its *rival*.[15] Where the language of the heart is used more restrictively for the affective dynamism of our subjective nature rather than our intellectual capacity to reflect what is really given in objective reality, then one would have to say that Newman's theology of revelation is *not* simply cordial. For him as for Augustine, the 'certainty of the ultimate rightness of the "true religion" does not rest', so Balthasar remarks, 'in mere intuitions of heart and conscience or of faith, but resides in a seeing of the rightness which in the broad sense must be called an aesthetic vision and yet which stands up to rational examination and ... can even be made visible to the person who purifies his mind's eye'.[16]

Newman's third kind of inspirational utility to Balthasar – after experiential holism and a vision, at once aesthetic and rational, of Christianity's 'rightness' – lies in the concept, central to the *Grammar of Assent*, worked out as that was in close connection with Balthasar's native city, of the convergence of evidence as illuminated by the illative sense. Reference to this notion opens and closes the seven volumes of Balthasar's theological aesthetics, beginning with his first sketch of the idea of revelatory form, *Gestalt*, as something that itself works on our human sensibility, our apparatus of possible response, and heightens its powers, and ending with his exposition of the New Testament's wonderful fulfilment of this notion, when the Word became flesh and we saw his Glory.

In the first volume of *Herrlichkeit*, we learn how through the convergence of evidence, as traced by the illative sense, a conclusion results as something suddenly seen – which is how Balthasar's Jesuit predecessor, Pierre Rousselot, in *Les yeux de la Foi* (over against the somewhat dessicatedly rationalistic apologetics of his time), understood the relation between the rational preamble of faith and faith's apprehension of God himself, revealing.[17] But then in the last volume, a biblical theology replicates the movement of faith in its own fashion; as it works through the data of the New Testament it shows in Balthasar's words, 'the "convergence" of the lines and paths of discernment ... on the single focal point of surpassing brightness, where the glory flares out'.[18]

That glory, in Balthasar's own idiom, is the 'absolute Trinitarian love of God, which discloses itself and offers itself in

Jesus Christ, which disarms by its humility and simplicity every "stronghold" of would-be mastering thought'[19] and in the substance of that claim no reader of Newman's *Parochial and Plain Sermons* is likely to drive a wedge between the Gospel preached at Littlemore and the Gospel from Lucerne. And then again in *Theodramatik*, where Balthasar is less concerned with the overall impression that Jesus made, the topic of theological aesthetics, and more with his saving action, that 'centre' discerned by illation is not so much displaced as re-described when he speaks of the 'ultimate lines of human destiny' as 'drawn to a transcendental point of convergence' in the *Resurrection* of Christ,[20] for the Crucified and Risen One *is* the Incarnate Word, just as the One who became incarnate did so in order by sacrificial death and exaltation to show his glory. Whether we are thinking in terms of theological aesthetics or theological dramatics, or, for that matter, theological logic, it is always the case (so Balthasar thought) that theological method should 'fold inwards ... towards the divine simplicity' – even though at the same time he also envisaged, significantly, a variety of theologies, grouped in two great families, the Greek and the Latin, being called to pursue that task in somewhat different ways. In an Eastern theology, each facet of the revelatory form is treated as transparent to its central epiphany, for the whole is transfigured by the divine glory. In a Western theology where doxology takes the different form of the bounden duty and service of rigorous thinking, revelation has many separate articulations in a variety of propositions and even treatises, but thought, if it is to be Christian, must nonetheless lead continually along these pathways to the midpoint Jesus Christ.

This notion, which at once licenses a plurality of theologies yet provides a criterion for their evaluation, brings me to the fourth and last general lesson Balthasar learnt from Newman, and, in this case, more specifically from Newman's Tractarian background. Typical of Newman, so Balthasar thought, was a pointing to the whole truth, whilst simultaneously renouncing system.[21] Despite Newman's priesthood and later cardinalate, Balthasar, in his discussion of theological styles, places him unhesitatingly with 'lay' rather than 'clerical' theology. Lay theology, in Balthasar's somewhat idiosyncratic use of that phrase, means a theology which refuses to limit itself either to pastoral concerns – practical usefulness to the Church's members – or to specialization of an academic kind, and which revolts against the narrowness that often afflicts Scholastic theology, linked as the latter is to the needs of basic ecclesiastical training in seminaries or official Church schools.[22] Balthasar's principal English example is Hopkins, but, he says, he could equally well have chosen either Newman or Chesterton.[23] Newman, he stresses, while insisting that the totality of revelation is so great that it can never be encompassed in one theological system, also considered that nonetheless theology should attempt to suggest that totality. In his theological aesthetics, in the course of considering Newman's influence on Hopkins, Balthasar emphasizes the need to integrate the imagination into the structure of thinking if such evocation of the revelatory totality is to succeed – and in this connection praises the *Grammar of Assent* for doing just that, locating it in a venerable tradition of Anglican divinity with just such an aim from Coleridge to Austin Farrer and Eric Mascall.[24] In the theological dramatics, by contrast, where Balthasar is concerned less with the response of the mind to the beauty of revelation and more with that of the will to its goodness, its saving power, he appeals again to what he takes to be the Newmanian idea that theology should evoke totality without ever claiming to englobe it – but this time in the context of the *freedom of the act of faith*. There can and should be 'pointers toward the ever-greater totality' which is revelation, and yet 'there must be no overwhelming proof, lest the freedom of the act of faith be over-ridden in a rationalistic way'.[25]

As Balthasar remarks, 'A method of proof that diminished the dramatic character of the Christ event would automatically show itself to be a failure',[26] and by this criterion, the method of the *Grammar of Assent* is a resounding success, confirming at the level of theological dramatic theory those credits which, when engaged on his project of theological aesthetics, he had already awarded it as a means, at once intellectual and aesthetic, of beginning to apprehend the divine transcendence in its embodied image, Jesus Christ.

Before leaving the general topic of Balthasar's overall indebtedness to Newman and considering more closely his attempt at a representation of the themes of the 1845 *Essay* I should, however, attempt to scotch one possible misunderstanding of Balthasar's claim that Newman's theology is essentially lay in style. He in no way meant by this that Newman's distinctive thought is somehow unsuited to the use of the *Amtskirche*, that part of the Church which through ordination exercises the apostolic ministry. Indeed, if we turn to the final volume of *Theologik*, the closing work of the entire trilogy, we find Newman's clerical ideal cited as an illustration of the personal holiness which should accompany the sacramental or institutional holiness of office of the priest. The Church of office, the Petrine church, requires the Church of love, the Johannine church: thus clerical holiness is not primarily a matter of moral duty but an expression of the unity which should hold good between what Balthasar terms the objective and subjective aspects of the economy of the Holy Spirit – the Spirit in institutions, the Spirit in hearts – his Christianized version of Hegel's distinction between objective and subjective *Geist* or mind.[27]

It is time to turn to those themes which most closely mirror the motifs of the *Essay on the Development of Christian Doctrine*. Were we in this regard simply to scour Balthasar's trilogy for explicit references to the *Essay on Development*, we should be disappointed. The *Grammar of Assent*, the *University Sermons*, the 'Preface' to the *Via Media*, *Difficulties of Anglicans*, the correspondence with the Abbé Jager, and even the reply to Peel in *The Tamworth Reading Room* figure more prominently. Surprising as it seems, given the extent of Newman's importance to Balthasar as I have charted it so far, Balthasar does not link the Oxford doctor by name with the idea of doctrinal development except in one rather cavalier reference, to be found in the extended essay on the Russian philosopher theologian Vladimir Sergeivić Solov'ev which forms part of the third volume of *Herrlichkeit*.[28] Let us polish off that morsel before tucking into the meat of this topic.

The association of Newman with Solov'ev would have encouraged those Anglican critics of Newman's *Essay* who considered that, despite his early strictures on Pusey's Germanophilia, he had sold out at the last to the evolutionary and organicist pretensions of German Idealism, so that the *Essay* led not so much to Rome as via Rome to Berlin and infidelity. Basing himself on Solov'ev's *Istoriya i budushchnost' teokratii* ('The History and Future of Theocracy'), written between 1885 and 1887 and, though not completed, published as a substantial fragment at Zagreb for fear of adverse reaction from the Tsarist censors, Balthasar identifies the central notion of Solov'ev's thought as process – a notion grounded in the intuition at the heart of German Idealism, but confirmed by the Russian thinker's research into cosmology, cultural history and the 'evolution of Christological truth in the dogmatic development of the Church – sketched by Solov'ev almost more painstakingly than by Newman'. Solov'ev inferred, in

Balthasar's summary, a 'progressive eschatological embodiment of the Divine Idea in worldly reality', and while the word 'Idea' here may remind us of a key term of the *Essay on Development*, the general conceptual idiom is evidently far removed from Newman's, putting us more in mind, perhaps, of what Chesterton called

> fantastic professors in fiction, who wave their hands and say, 'Thus do we mount to the ineffable heights of pure and radiant Being'; or, worse still, of actual professors in real life, who say, 'All Being is Becoming; and is but the evolution of Not-Being by the law of its Being'[29]

– a reference to the Neo-Hegelianism fashionable in Chesterton's early manhood, not least at Oxford. I must not, however, be unfair to Solov'ev, whose treatise, with its account of the delicate equilibrium of the mutually defining offices of king, prophet and priest in a Christian society, is more than a little reminiscent, at any rate in its formal structure, of the 'Preface' to the *Via Media*.[30] But a Balthasarian re-statement of the themes of the 1845 *Essay* does not lie in this direction.

To arrive at that re-statement by counting references to Newman will not serve, for it lies in the integration, conscious or unconscious, of Newmanian motifs in the deep structure of Balthasar's theological thought. There are three of these, and they resolve ultimately into claims about, respectively, Jesus, Mary and Peter.

The single most important contribution of Balthasar's work to a theological understanding of the *Essay* concerns the notion of objective revelatory form, central as that is to the theological aesthetics, which aesthetics are themselves, on Balthasar's own account, the necessary prolegomena to theological dramatics, for we must grasp the Word of God in human guise if we are to respond to the action which it undertakes on the world-stage – the whole finding its culmination in the theological logic which considers what truth must be if the divine beauty and its saving goodness are really given us through the historic revelation, *really* given us, or as we say in conversational English, given us really *and truly*. The notion of the objective form of revelation, in other words, plays the same pivotal role in Balthasar's theological vision as does that of the Christian 'Idea' in Newman's *Essay*. But more than that: the two notions are not just similarly important; they are also similar *tout court*. Or to put it more provocatively, it was to this concept of the objective revelatory form of the Gospel that Newman's mind and sensibility reached out, without ever quite giving it adequate articulation. The 'objective existence' of Christianity, its 'historically unmistakable and bold outlines', history's 'imprinting on our minds' Christianity's 'living image': once the student of Newman has read the opening volume of Balthasar's *Herrlichkeit – Schau der Gestalt, Seeing the Form*, these phrases taken from Newman's own 'Introduction' to his *Essay* will never, I venture to predict, be separable henceforth from that key idea of theological aesthetics.[31] And how could we miss, after immersion in Balthasar, the aesthetic model underlying this crucial statement in the *Essay*'s opening chapter 'On the Development of Ideas':

> Ideas are not ordinarily brought home to the mind, except through the medium of a variety of aspects; like bodily substances, which are not seen except under the clothing of their properties and influences, and can be walked round and surveyed on opposite sides and in different perspectives and in contrary lights. And as views of a material object may be taken from points so remote or so distinct that they seem at first sight incompatible, and especially as their shadows will be disproportionate or even monstrous, and yet all these will be harmonised together by taking account of the point of vision or the surface of projection, so also all the representations of an idea, even all the misrepresentations, are capable of mutual reconciliation and adjustment, and of a resolution into the subject to which they belong, and their contrariety, when explained, is an argument for its substantiveness and integrity, and their variety for its originality and power.[32]

Or as Balthasar puts it, 'the unity of the form offers a fullness of approaches, doors and possibilities for entry'.[33] In those words from the concluding volume of *The Glory of the Lord*, Balthasar applies to the biblical revelation with its centre in Christ, as to a surpassingly pre-eminent case, what in the opening volume of *Theologik*, in a description of the truth of reality at large, he has said of *any* significant form. The human mind draws from the imaged world around us *eine Ganzheit der Gestalt*, a 'wholeness of form', whereby our shifting perceptions of things come to appear as so many presentations, from different angles, of the same reality.[34] The greater the intrinsic significance of the form – in Newman's vocabulary, the *idea* – the more varied the perspectives it provokes and offers to our gaze.

Where Balthasar's account *adds* to what Newman left us is his insistence that, however many *aspects* the idea may manifest, however many 'perspects' – *perspectives* – it may permit, it retains a unity which transcends all of them thanks to its possession of an organizing centre. And this midpoint of the form is *Jesus Christ himself.* In his capacity to enable the intersection of a multitude of relationships, vertical and horizontal, to past and to future, he constitutes himself, in his life, death and Resurrection, the indispensable reference point of all theology and all contemplation worthy of the Christian name. A putative doctrinal development, therefore, will be able to establish its claim, if and only if it can show that it forms a connection in the total nexus of relations of which Christ is the centre – whether or not this was explicitly recognized by the witnesses of the apostolic generation themselves. Such a Christological re-casting of Newman's 'divine Idea' has the merit among others of aligning Newman's account more fully with what is now the most authoritative statement of the Catholic communion on this subject – the Dogmatic Constitution *Dei Verbum*, on Divine Revelation, of the Second Vatican Council, where speaking precisely of the 'inner unity' of the 'plan of revelation', Christ is declared to be simultaneously revelation's Mediator *and its fullness.*[35] I have showed elsewhere that this text was almost certainly indebted to the Christocentric view of doctrinal development worked out by Balthasar's colleague and friend Henri de Lubac, who sought to inject into the narrower topic of the development of doctrine a shot of that Christ-centredness which, in the steps of Barth, Balthasar tried to revive in the Catholic theology of revelation as a whole.[36] It is by coming to see some facet of the revelatory form in its relation to that form's midpoint that one comes to register what Newman calls in the *Essay* its 'due shape and complete proportions'.[37]

I come now to the second principal motif relevant to the *Essay on Development*, and that concerns the mode in which such theologically aesthetic perception of shape and proportion, in Newman's words, 'spreads through a community and attains general reception'.[38] A major harbinger of the *Essay* had been the 1843 Sermon on 'The Theory of Developments in Religious Doctrine' where Newman had put forward as an archetype of the Church developing doctrine the Blessed Virgin Mary, as she appears in the Lucan infancy Gospel, ruminating, turning over in her mind, the impression left by the childhood of Christ. *Dei Verbum*, once again, takes up this Marian perspective in its own brief theology of development when it ascribes 'growth in the understanding of the realities and the words ... handed down' (in Tradition) to, in the first place, the 'contemplation and study made by believers, who treasure these things in their hearts and through the intimate understanding of spiritual things they experience'.[39] What Balthasar provides is a fuller dogmatic understanding of why all development of doctrine can usefully be regarded as issuing from this Marian matrix.

For Balthasar, Mary's faith-response to the incarnating Word constitutes a kind of *a priori* structure – to use the language of Kantian epistemology – governing the corporate faith of the entire subsequent Church. It is, to his mind, a presupposition of the Incarnation that there should be, within the purely human realm, a receiving subject to whom the final revelation could be made in more than simply an approximative way. As he writes:

> Somewhere, in the name of all mankind, a *fiat* with no internal boundaries must exist in response to the final word of God that continually transcends all understanding, a *fiat* that goes all the way to the end with God's Word in unreserved agreement, in the meditative attempt to understand [and at this point Balthasar involves the same Lucan texts indicated by Newman in the sermon of 1843]; ... and this [so Balthasar continues, with reference now to the development of doctrine in the Church of Christ born from Mary's faith] *sets in motion an endless historical process.*[40]

Thanks to the 'Marian principle', as Balthasar terms it, the entire later Church lives from this Marian matrix. As the God-bearer who is such precisely through her faith, Mary 'encloses all Christians within herself and brings them forth from herself along with their experience of faith'.[41] As Mary's 'archetypal' experience passes over into the 'imitative' experience of the Church's members, the privileges of personal intimacy with Christ as a result of which she enjoyed the tact which enabled her to judge rightly of her Son, centre-point of revelation as he is, are gradually expropriated (in Balthasar's key term) in favour of ordinary believers. And this, for Balthasar, explains the prophetical office of the Church, or more precisely the prophetical tradition to which Newman contrasted – though in no contestational spirit – the episcopal tradition in the 1837 treatise on that subject. To Balthasar that contrast is not so much a revindication of the rights of the Christian laity as a way of speaking about the dramatic interplay between the mystical Church, the *ecclesia Mariana*, and the Church of office, the Church of Peter.[42]

And that way of speaking – with Newman, with Balthasar – of the inter-relation of the *sensus Ecclesiae* and the magisterium brings me in conclusion to the third motif of the idea of development re-worked in Swiss perspective, and that concerns the Petrine teaching-office which, in the manner of the early Cyprian, Balthasar ascribes to the entire Catholic episcopate – while reserving, of course, a quite special place for the Roman church and bishop in this regard. In the *Essay on Development* Newman wrote, 'If Christianity is both social and dogmatic, and intended for all ages, it must, humanly speaking, have an infallible expounder.'[43]

From the late 1850s to the late 1870s Newman would be preoccupied by the need to do justice to the role of the laity on the one hand and that of the Roman pontiff on the other in the expository process. In the Marian church, the living faith of the believer, remarks Balthasar, echoing Newman, has regard to

> a totality of fulness which the believer can discern through the Holy Spirit, at least to the extent that, while he can never attain an overview of it, he can detect every substantial omission from it as a violation of the law of the whole, of inner proportion, or, rather, of the law of God's self-giving, which is 'always more'.[44]

The *magisterium externum* of episcopal tradition in the Church of Peter exists to serve the holism of this instinct of faith in the *magisterium internum* of prophetic tradition in the Church of Mary.[45] Like a seismographic instrument (Balthasar's simile), the teaching office will react when some 'substantial underground tremor threatens the totality or catholicity of revelation'.[46] The task of that office is to re-create the inner harmony of the Gospel's organic unity when through some distorting unilateralism of emphasis it gets upset. Balthasar accurately reflects Newman's concern in the 'Preface' to the *Via Media* that the pope and his curia should not attempt to replace the function of the theologian in the schools. Yet his explanation of their inter-relation, I venture to say, improves on Newman's, in stressing that 'the teaching-office is not primarily concerned with the formulation but with the charge it bears [for "the same proposition can bear a different charge in the mouth of Augustine and in that of Jansen"]. Its particular definitions and condemnations are always made with a view to re-establishing the endangered totality.'[47] Balthasar preserves the pastoral finality of magisterial inventions which led Newman to attribute those interventions to the regal office of the

Church, but at the same time does not separate them from the teaching office – the prophetic office of the Church in its specifically episcopal form, which we must surely regard as the inconvenience, the implausibility indeed, of Newman's version.

Newman wrote to his brother Francis, 'I have been sent into Switzerland to be made young again'.[48] Another master of singing school would follow him to finish a lament for the decrepitude not of an individual but of Christendom's civilization. But if Eliot, finishing *The Waste Land* at Lausanne in 1922, could end nonetheless on a note of hope, in the Sanskrit invocation of a peace that passes all understanding, how much the more, for those whose life is theologically grounded, can there be hope of rejuvenescence for that Church and faith which Newman embraced at such cost in 1845. Balthasar's theological achievement, with its confidence that the Gospel can salve the wounds, untangle the contradictions, and lift the limitations, of contemporary culture shows us that Pentecostal grace has not lost its freshness in our time. Not the least aspect of that *recursus ad fontes* lies in Balthasar's encouragement that we should look at Newman with the originality as well as fidelity Newman himself brought to the faith of the Church. An 'idea' may 'develop', showing new sides of itself, if only we view Littlemore from Lucerne.

Notes

1. Cited in J. Wraight, *The Swiss and the British* (Wilton, Salisbury, 1987), p. 227.
2. J. Gage, *J. M. W. Turner: 'A Wonderful Range of Mind'* (New Haven and London, 1987), p. 243.
3. J. Ruskin, *Modern Painters* (Orpington, 1888), V, p. 362 (from the Epilogue to the last edition published in Ruskin's lifetime).
4. Cited in A. Lunn, *Switzerland and the English* (London, 1944), p. 42.
5. Ruskin noted the frequency with which Turner sketched the Rigi: see I. Warrell, *Through Switzerland with Turner: Ruskin's First Selection from the Turner Bequest* (London, 1995), p. 75. Newman refused to go up it: C. S. Dessain, Cong.Orat. (ed.), *John Henry Newman, Letters and Diaries* XXII (London, 1972), p. 285. Cited below as *LD* XXII.
6. C. S. Dessain, Cong.Orat., and T. Gornall, SJ (eds), *John Henry Newman, Letters and Diaries* XXV (Oxford, 1973), p. 199.
7. Cited in J. Wraight, *The Swiss and the British*, p. 219.
8. J. L. Schiffmann, *Lebengeschichte Alois Güglers* (Augsburg, 1833).
9. For an overview, see D. Gla, *Repertorium der katholisch-theologischen Literatur in Deutschland, Oesterreich und der Schweiz*, I, 1 (Paderborn, 1895).
10. H. U. von Balthasar, *The Glory of the Lord: A Theological Aesthetics, I: Seeing the Form* (ET, Edinburgh, 1982), pp. 94–104. Cited below as *GL* I.
11. *Ibid.*, p. 354.
12. H. U. von Balthasar, *Theologik. III: Der Geist der Wahrheit* (Einsiedeln, 1987), p. 292. Cited below as *TL* III.

13. 'Immediate contact': in the context of the natural knowledge of God, which is chiefly at issue in the *Grammar of Assent*, this might be thought to raise the issue of Ontologism. Balthasar cites elsewhere, relevantly, Erich Przywara's defence of Newman's illative sense: 'There is no direct intuition of the primal divine Ground, even if the "conclusion" expresses itself psychologically as direct perception. This is an inchoate kind of knowledge, but in it, nonetheless, the divine is grasped as the Absolute, the Ground . . . of all that is in the world.' (*Theo-drama: IV: The Action* (ET, San Francisco, 1994), p. 141, with reference to Przywara's *Religionsbegründung* (Freiburg, 1923)).

14. *GL* I, p. 515. Balthasar characterizes this approach in general in this way:

> This theology was in a new way an elevation and fulfilment of metaphysics, be-cause explicitly and for the first time it knew how to explain *ontologically* the *ontic* (historical) event of salvation. It was historical inasmuch as it revealed to concrete man (in his condition of guilt and death) where and how transcendence is to be found. It was personal inasmuch as only *one* concrete man (and not abstract neu-tral human nature) could be the subject of this self-abandonment and agony, in personal love for a personal God. At the same time it was universal inasmuch as his unique self-giving and suffering opened up for all access to complete tran-scendence in the form of salvation. (*The Glory of the Lord, V: The Realm of Metaphysics in the Modern Age* (ET, Edinburgh, 1991), p. 51)

15. *GL* I, p. 167.

16. H. U. von Balthasar, *The Glory of the Lord. A Theological Aesthetics. II. Studies in Theological Styles: Clerical Styles* (ET, Edinburgh, 1984), p. 139. Cited below as *GL* II.

17. *GL* I, p. 176.

18. H. U. von Balthasar, *The Glory of the Lord. A Theological Aesthetics VII: Theology: the New Covenant* (ET, Edinburgh, 1989), p. 18. Cited below as *GL* VII.

19. *Ibid.*, p. 15: 'stronghold' refers to the *ochyrōmata*, fortresses of worldly thought which would obstruct the knowledge of God in 2 Cor. 10.4–5.

20. H. U. von Balthasar, *Theo-drama. Theological Dramatic Theory. II: The Dramatis Personae: Man in God* (ET, San Francisco, 1990), p. 94. Cited below as *TD* II.

21. *GL* II, p. 25.

22. *Ibid.*, p. 16.

23. *Ibid.*, p. 21.

24. H. U. von Balthasar, *The Glory of the Lord. A Theological Aesthetics III: Studies in Theological Styles: Lay Styles* (ET, Edinburgh, 1986), pp. 353–4. Cited below as *GL* III.

25. *TD* II, p. 130.

26. *Ibid.*, p. 115.

27. *TL* III, p. 322.

28. *GL* III, p. 283.

29. G. K. Chesterton, *St Thomas Aquinas* (London, 1933), pp. 180–1.

30. See for instance the exposition of the 'inter-dependent nature of their functions and authority' in J. Sutton, *The Religious Philosophy of Vladimir Solovyov. Towards a Reassessment* (London, 1988), p. 86.

31. J. H. Newman, *An Essay on the Development of Christian Doctrine. The Essay of 1845* (Harmondsworth, 1973), pp. 69, 72, 74. Cited below as *ED*.

32. *Ibid.*, p. 95.

33. *GL* VII, p. 15.

34. H. U. von Balthasar, *Theologik I: Wahrheit der Welt* (Einsiedeln, 1985), p. 147.

35. *Dei Verbum* 2.

36. A. Nichols, OP, *From Newman to Congar. The Idea of Doctrinal Development from the Victorians to the Second Vatican Council* (Edinburgh, 1990), pp. 195–213.

37. *ED*, p. 109.

38. *Ibid.*

39. *Dei Verbum* 8.

40. *GL* VII, p. 94. Italics added.

41. *GL* I, p. 340.
42. H. U. von Balthasar, *Theo-drama III: The Dramatis Personae: The Person in Christ* (ET, San Francisco, 1992), p. 358.
43. *ED*, p. 177.
44. *TD* II, pp. 99–100.
45. *TL* III, p. 302.
46. *Ibid.*, p. 101.
47. *Ibid.*
48. *LD* XXII, p. 299.

8

The Anthropology of Conversion: Newman and the Contemporary Theology of Religions

Terrence Merrigan

Introduction: The Theology of Religions in a Postmodern Context

It is by now something of a commonplace to describe Newman as the 'invisible peritus' of the Second Vatican Council, and to regard at least some of its teaching as a vindication of both his theological instincts and his theological options.[1] One thinks in this regard of, among other things, his views on the role of the laity in the Church, his defence of the freedom of conscience, his sensitivity in matters ecumenical and his concern that the Church take seriously the challenges and the opportunities thrown up by the ever-changing historical context.[2] However, as a number of theologians have indicated, the world into which Vatican II was born and which received it with such enthusiasm was far different from the world we now inhabit. Vatican II, it might be said, was the product and the expression of the Church's attempt to come to terms with modernity. Indeed, one of its most significant documents, *Gaudium et Spes*, was explicitly focused on the place of the Church in the modern world.

But the modern world is no more. Modernity has given way to postmodernity. Postmodernity has been described as the radicalization of the insights and achievements of modernity. Among the many features of modernity which might be highlighted, I would like to reflect on three which are particularly relevant to my subject matter here.

Modernity meant insight into our *historicity*. Postmodernity means the dizzying recognition that everything we hold dear, even our value systems and religious traditions, is subject to the permutations of history, is characterized, in other words, by a far-reaching *relativity*. This recognition can issue in either an indifferent relativism or a hermeneutics of hope which seeks critically to reappropriate our cultural and religious traditions.[3]

Modernity meant the determination to subject any and all claims to knowledge to the test of experimental or *empirical investigation*. Postmodernity means that *experience* is the measure of all things, the fundamental criterion determining all judgements. The decision to accord experience such a central role in the formulation of truth-claims and value-judgements can issue in either paralysing subjectivism or the quest for a communally agreed and communally verifiable norm for commitment and action.

Modernity meant the respectful recognition and tolerance of *difference*. Postmodernity means a determination to celebrate *otherness*, that is to say, to take seriously and to open oneself to the particular experience of hitherto marginalized constituencies, such as women, or social and sexual minorities. This openness to alterity can issue either in vacuous imitation of, or critical engagement with, the other. In the latter case, there is a willingness to learn from the other, coupled with a determination to challenge that other in the name of one's own tradition.[4]

I noted at the outset that Newman's theology anticipated the thought of Vatican II. It was therefore relevant to the concerns of modernity. Newman the empiricist,[5] Newman the historian of doctrinal development, and Newman the searcher of his own inner life are all at home in the modern age. But does Newman have anything to say to postmodernity, characterized as it is by its preoccupation with personal experience, its ominous sense of the relativity of all traditions, and its acute sensitivity to the 'other'?

In what follows I would like to reflect on this question by confronting Newman with a distinctly postmodern theological problem, namely, the problem of the plurality of religious traditions, or, more positively expressed, the question of interreligious dialogue.

It is not surprising that the theology of religions finds itself in the front lines of the debate about postmodernity.

Much that is fundamental to Christianity seems to be incompatible with the postmodern ethos. In opposition to the postmodern valuation of present experience, Christianity finds its raison d'être in the biblical history of an itinerant Jewish preacher

of the first century. In opposition to the postmodern determination to accord the other equal status with oneself, Christianity
insists that Jesus of Nazareth is the definitive[6] and normative
means to salvation. In opposition to the postmodern sensitivity to
the relative character of all traditions, Christianity claims that its
faith tradition is possessed of universal significance.

These are all claims which John Henry Newman, and the
Council with which his name is most associated, unequivocally
endorsed. Do they have a place in the current theological debate?
This is the matter I would like to discuss in the following pages.
I would propose to do this as follows.

First, I will sketch the views of that school of theology which is
most sympathetic to postmodern sensibilities, and, at first sight,
most removed from Newman, namely, the so-called pluralist
school.

Second, I will sketch the views of Vatican II and of the postconciliar Catholic theology of religions, the so-called inclusivist
school.

In a third section, I will endeavour to isolate Newman's own
theology of religions and religious conversion, and to relate this
to both the pluralist and contemporary Catholic theology of religions.

Finally, in a summary conclusion, I will reflect briefly on the
themes of experience, alterity and relativity in Newman's theology
of religions.

It is my view that Newman's portrayal of the 'natural religion'
which exists outside the Judaeo-Christian dispensation is not
completely foreign to the postmodern sensibility. Moreover, it
can serve as a corrective both to contemporary pluralist and inclusivist views.

The Pluralist Theology of Religions

The Term 'Pluralist'

The so-called pluralist school of theologians, represented by,
among others, John Hick, Paul Knitter and Wilfred Cantwell
Smith, has largely set the current theological agenda, as far as the
theology of religions is concerned. The pluralists are united in
their willingness to take leave of the traditional claim regarding
the definitive character (or 'superiority', as it is sometimes called),
of Christ and Christianity. At the same time, they affirm the 'independent validity of other ways' to salvation.[7]

Pluralism here clearly means more than the mere juxtaposition of divergent religious traditions. According to Langdon Gilkey, the term 'pluralism', as used by pluralist theologians, acquires a new dimension, namely, that of parity (or, at least, of 'rough parity').[8] A pluralist, in the modern sense of the word, acknowledges, not always without regret, that other religions and other saviours can be as efficacious as Christianity.

In 1988, the pluralist theologians published what might be described as the 'pluralist manifesto'. *The Myth of Christian Uniqueness*[9] brings together some of the best and brightest of those theologians who share the view that, in our radically pluralistic world, only an equally radical pluralist theology of religions can do justice to the world's religious traditions and, indeed, to Christianity itself.

In his preface to the collection, Knitter distinguishes the pluralistic approach to the theology of religions from the two traditional Christian approaches. The pluralist paradigm rejects outright the conservative, exclusivistic model (*exclusivism*) which cannot conceive of salvation apart from an explicit faith in the Christ. But it also aims to go beyond the more liberal, inclusivistic model (*inclusivism*) – the model associated especially with Karl Rahner and implicitly espoused by Vatican II – which acknowledges the positive role played by other religious traditions, but regards Christ as the ultimate source and/or normative symbol of all salvation, and conceives of explicit Christian faith as the completion of every religious system.[10]

Pluralism and Present Religious Experience
The pluralist paradigm seems particularly well suited to our postmodern age.

In the first place, it places a premium on *present religious experience*, as opposed to historical revelation. For the pluralists, the notion of revelation, understood as a distinctive act of self-disclosure, on the part of God, to a particular individual or people, is intrinsically reprehensible.

The pluralist deity is determinedly democratic. In the words of one advocate of the pluralist paradigm,

> the pluralist position envisions a fairer God who gives equal opportunity for ultimate fulfilment to persons of all major religions ... Pluralism ... does not hold one religion to be more privileged than others. It does not claim that God is (metaphorically) personally involved in only one religion, namely, Christianity. God is

present to and immanent in all the world religions. This presence of God is manifest differently through the various scriptures, prophets and sages of the religions.[11]

Pluralism, so to speak, extends the revelatory franchise to all the great post-axial traditions.[12]

From the pluralist perspective, the world's religious *traditions* represent the culturally-conditioned expressions of a universally accessible religious experience.[13] That experience is, of course, always shaped by the cultural and religious context within which it takes place. In this sense, there is no such thing as 'pure' religious experience, and pluralists rightly reject the charge that they regard particular religious traditions as, so to speak, 'accessories after the religious fact'. The concrete religious traditions provide the forum within which religious experience becomes possible, and the categories which allow believers both to express that experience and, most importantly, to identify its source or its ground.

The *founders* of the post-axial religious traditions were inspired religious leaders who enjoyed 'powerful and persistent' religious experiences of unusual intensity.[14] For those who follow in their footsteps, 'the way to salvation/liberation involves a gradual or sudden conversion to [the] new way of experiencing' the self and the world disclosed by the founder. However, in the case of 'ordinary believers, the new mode of experiencing usually occurs only occasionally and is of only moderate intensity'.[15]

The '*object*' of religious experience has many names, depending on which tradition one consults. It may be conceived of as personal or impersonal, as possessed of a distinctive character (a loving Father) or as utterly formless (a Void).[16] Pluralists are quick to point out that all the world's great religions contain an apophatic tradition, often mystic in character, which insists that the Godhead, as it is in itself, is utterly beyond categorization or description. It seems that pluralist theologians regard these apophatic traditions as something akin to empirical proof, so to speak, of one of their fundamental theological axioms, namely, that the Absolute cannot be identified with, much less confined to, any particular religious tradition.

Pluralism and the Relativity of Religious Traditions

The insistence on the ultimately mysterious character of the Absolute explains pluralism's compatibility with the second feature of the postmodern ethos which we sketched above, namely, the insistence on the relative character of all cultural and religious traditions. The ultimate elusiveness of religion's object makes it difficult to conceive of religious traditions as, in any meaningful sense, depositories or transmitters of religious 'knowledge'. Strictly speaking, they are no more (but also no less) than tried and proven 'responses' to the Transcendent.

This feature of pluralism is well reflected in John Hick's approach to Christ. For Hick, Jesus' religious significance consists, above all, in his role as exemplar or model, that is to say, his role as a concrete realisation of 'one valid way among others of conceptualizing and responding to the divine'. Jesus' contemporary appeal consists precisely in his 'universally relevant religious experience' and his 'ethical insights', provided that 'these are freed from the mass of ecclesiastical dogmas and practices that have developed over the centuries, reflecting cultures as widely different from ours as the Roman empire and medieval Christianity'. For Hick, 'all the great religious figures have in their different ways "incarnated" the ideal of human life lived in response to the divine Reality'.[17] 'Christianity is one among a plurality of authentic responses to the divine reality.'[18]

Pluralism and Alterity

Pluralism makes a virtue out of the *otherness* of the world's many religious traditions. Since every particular religious tradition, Christianity included, provides us with 'only' a qualified 'knowledge' of the religious object, it is in the interest of every tradition that its qualified 'knowledge' be supplemented, if not corrected, by the insights of other traditions. Once the partial character of all truth-claims has been established, the problem of rival truth-claims can be readily addressed. As far as the religious object itself is concerned, such claims are best regarded as complementary. (This issues in a view of religious truth as polar.[19]) As far as the reciprocal relations among the world's religious traditions are concerned, dialogue presents itself as the only rationally and religiously defensible option. (This issues in an appeal to believers in all traditions to engage in the practice of 'crossing-over' from one tradition to another.[20]) As far as the reconciliation of rival doctrinal traditions is concerned, believers are invited to tolerate differences, to acknowledge the ultimately mysterious character of the religious object, and to recognize that all religions are already united in sharing a common soteriological concern. As one author, S. Mark Heim, has recently observed, it is striking that,

'in expositions of pluralistic theologies of religion by their primary advocates, one word never appears in the plural: salvation'.
The same author goes on to remark that 'this is the more dramatic
since diversity is otherwise their constant theme'. Among the pluralist theologians, and in spite of their commitment to diversity,
' "salvation" remains a comfortable and unitary reference point'.
It serves as 'the universal, cross-cultural constant in interpreting
religious traditions'. For the pluralists, Heim explains, 'salvation'
is 'shorthand for one process taking place within all major religious traditions, though not normatively understood or described
in any of them'.[21] Hick, for example, describes the salvific goal
shared by the great world religions as 'the realization of a limit-
lessly better possibility' of human existence through the pro-
motion of 'the transformation of human existence from
self-centredness to Reality-centredness'.[22] (This issues in the so-
called soteriocentric approach to interreligious dialogue, that is to
say, the determination to focus not on doctrinal differences but
on the soteriological project which all the major religions are
thought to espouse).[23]

Contemporary Catholic Theology of Religions

Vatican II on the Mediation of Salvation

Clearly, the pluralist theology of religions represents a radical departure from traditional approaches. Pluralist theologians are well
aware of this fact. They are inclined to describe their methodo-
logical option as the crossing of a theological Rubicon.[24] Pluralist
theologians do not hide their conviction that coming to terms
with the contemporary context[25] also means, for Christianity, a
coming of age. In their view, the future of Christianity can only
be guaranteed by a radical break with the confessional past. An
adult Christianity, a postmodern Christianity, cannot take its
lessons from the past. It must take its lead from the contemporary context.

The Catholic Church does not have a very good track record
as far as attention to the contemporary context is concerned. As I
have indicated, it was only in 1962, with the convocation of
Vatican II, that the Church signalled its willingness to come to
grips with the modern world. It has been suggested that this was
much too late, that the Church engaged modernity just as modernity was drawing to a close. The current trends in the theology of
religions, at least as represented by the pluralist approach, would

seem to support this judgement. At first sight, official Catholic teaching on the non-Christian religions seems rather far removed from both the postmodern ethos and pluralist proposals.

Vatican II squarely adopts an 'inclusivist' approach to other religions, which seems to leave little room for an unconditional valuation of their particular religious experience or their distinctiveness, and which does not appear to reflect a willingness to relativize Christianity's own claims and traditions.

Inclusivism is perhaps best seen as a theology of religions which is characterized, above all, by a preoccupation with the concrete mediation of salvation, that is to say, with the way in which human beings come to know of and share in God's salvific will. At the risk of oversimplification, we might suggest that this concern with *mediation* distinguishes inclusivism from exclusivism which focuses, above all, on the *mediator*, Christ, and from pluralism which focuses, above all, on the *object* of humanity's religious quest.

Inclusivism is founded on the paradox of universality and particularity. It struggles to maintain a balance between the universalism implied in the claim that God desires the salvation of all persons (1 Tim. 2.4), and the scandal of particularity contained in the claim that this salvation has been realized in the contingent history of Jesus of Nazareth and is carried on in the checkered history of the church.

This paradox or polar tension is the source of a fundamental ambiguity in Catholic teaching on the non-Christian religions, an ambiguity which Vatican II did not (and perhaps could not) overcome. On the one hand, the Council unequivocally endorsed the view (which has a long and complicated history) that those who are not actual members of the Church, and even professed atheists, can be saved.[26] On the other hand, the Council is insistent that Christ 'is "the way, the truth and the life" (John 14.16), ... in whom God has reconciled all things to himself',[27] and that the Church is the 'universal sacrament of salvation'.[28]

The Council portrays the world's religions primarily as manifestations of, and responses to, the perplexity of men and women in the face of what the Council describes as 'the obscure riddles of the human condition which today also, as in the past, profoundly disturb their hearts'. These riddles include such questions as:

> What is a human being? What is the meaning and purpose of life? What is good and what is sin? What origin and purpose do suf-

ferings have? What is the way to attaining true happiness? ...
What is that final unutterable mystery which takes in our lives
and from which we take our origin and towards which we tend?²⁹

The Council insists that 'the catholic church rejects nothing of
those things which are true and holy' in the world's great religious
traditions. Indeed, it professes to 'regard with respect those ways
of acting and living and those precepts and teachings which,
though often at variance with what it holds and expounds, fre-
quently reflect a ray of that truth which enlightens everyone'.³⁰
At no point, however, does the Council describe the non-
Christian religions as 'revealed'.³¹ The Council's most important
pronouncement on the non-Christian religions, *Nostra Aetate* (28
October 1965) or the *Declaration on the Church's Relation to Non-
Christian Religions* is more significant for the fact of its appearance than for its content. It signalled a new attitude (*habitudo*) on
the part of the Church towards the other religions and a new willingness to recognize their positive contribution to humanity's religious quest. However, neither here nor elsewhere does the
Council provide a theology of the non-Christian religions, that is
to say, a critical reflection on their nature and their place in the
economy of salvation.³²

Post-Conciliar Inclusivism

This task was assumed by theologians after the Council (though,
of course, the new conciliar openness had itself been prepared by
the work of theologians, and of Karl Rahner in particular). Since
the Council, Catholic theologians have come to accord the non-
Christian religions an ever more positive role in God's plan of salvation. These religions are now regarded, at the very least, as the
visible social expression both of the human quest for God and of
God's will to draw all men and women to Himself. Some theologians even go further and view the non-Christian religions,
understood as social entities characterized by ritual, and belief
and ethical systems, as the ordinary or normal channels, within
which, for the great majority of humankind, God's universal
salvific will is expressed and even engaged (so Hans Küng and
Heinz Robert Schlette).³³
It would, however, be misleading to conclude that the Christ-
event has, in any sense, been relativized by these developments.
For Catholic inclusivism, Christ is always implicated in the salvific process, either as the *font* of saving grace (including that

grace which is operative in the non-Christian religions), or as the *goal* of all of humanity's religious striving (in which case he is the norm against which all religious systems are to be measured), or as the *catalyst* for the operation of 'the Spirit of truth' who fills all of creation and draws all women and men to the Father (via diverse religious traditions).[34]

It is the claim regarding the overarching significance of Christ which makes inclusivism so objectionable to pluralist theologians. Such Christocentrism, it is argued, reduces other religions to the role of bit-players in the drama of salvation. From the pluralist perspective, the *a priori* insistence on Christ's centrality to the economy of salvation makes genuine interreligious dialogue impossible, since the other traditions are not respected in their integral 'otherness'. That 'otherness' includes the steadfast conviction of non-Christians that their religions constitute independently valid ways of salvation. These ways clearly bear the marks of the context within which they originated and are, to that degree, historically and culturally relative. Nonetheless, they constitute forums within which authentic religious experience is possible, and by means of which men and women are salvifically related to the Godhead.

Clearly, the progress made in the Catholic theology of religions since Vatican II, under the impetus of the conciliar teaching, bears witness to the fact that inclusivism is by no means moribund. Whether it is up to the challenges of postmodernity has yet to be decided. It is obvious that the conciliar teaching as such cannot be the final word. But then again, it was never intended to be. Reflecting on the conciliar teaching, and on recent Catholic theology of religions, one wonders whether the inclusivist approach can yield perhaps even more fruit than it has up to now. In other words, can the inclusivist paradox more adequately accommodate postmodern concerns than even recent developments suggest?

It is in the light of this query that we turn our attention to the 'invisible *peritus*' of Vatican II and his reflections on religion and religious conversion.

Newman's Theology of Religions and Religious Conversion

The locus in Newman's writings for his 'theology of religions' is above all his discussion, in the *Grammar of Assent*, of what he describes as the 'natural religion' founded on the experience of conscience. The theme of conversion occupies a central place in this discussion. By conversion, I mean the process whereby the individual, under the impulse of a divine call, turns from 'self' towards the Creator from whom he or she expects salvation. This turning, this *metanoia*, finds expression in ever more profound devotional and ethical praxis.

Alongside his many reservations about natural religion – and I shall have occasion to mention these – Newman also displays a genuine regard for the achievements and character of what he describes as the 'dispensation of paganism'. We do him no injustice, I think, when we examine his writings with a view to extracting the more positive elements of his analysis. Indeed, we do no more than theologians have always done when, in their attempt to come to terms with a new cultural and intellectual context, they reappropriate their theological and doctrinal tradition. We need not do violence to Newman's treatment of natural religion to reappropriate it in a constructive way, that is to say, in a way which will enable Newman's theology to contribute to the contemporary debate.

I have fixed on the theme of conversion as a major element in Newman's understanding of natural religion. I would like to reflect on this very broad theme from three angles: (1) the origin and expression of the call to conversion; (2) the character of the God of conversion; and (3) the anthropological reality of conversion.

Newman's treatment of these themes contains valuable lessons for both pluralists and inclusivists. At the same time, Newman's reflections would appear to be in line with those postmodern themes we described at the outset, namely, (1) the valuation of human experience, (2) the demand to respect 'otherness', and (3) the recognition of the relative character of all cultural and religious traditions.

In what follows, I shall attempt both to clarify Newman's contribution to the contemporary theology of religions, and to highlight his compatibility with our postmodern ethos.

The Origin and Expression of the Call to Conversion (Inclusivism, Experience and the Character of Natural Religion)

As is well known, Newman develops his understanding of natural religion out of his doctrine of conscience.[35] The experience of conscience is, in Newman's view, a universal phenomenon, a

'mental act' constitutive of our self-conscious life in the same way,
and with the same claim to authenticity as memory, sensation and
reasoning.[36] Newman described the experience of conscience as
the '*feeling* of ... right and wrong under a special sanction' (emphasis in original).[37] The sanction, which Newman describes as
'the sense of a particular judgement [whether prohibitive or hor-
tatory] ... on the quality of [a specific] action' is always attended
by certain distinct emotions.[38] These emotions are vital to the experience of conscience. Their presence implies an Invisible Being
both exterior and superior to ourselves, with whom we are in immediate relation, 'One to whom we are responsible, before whom
we are ashamed, whose claims we fear'.[39] Only a 'living object', an
'intelligent being', could excite in us those feelings of remorse or
satisfaction – those 'emotions' – which are an integral part of our
experience of conscience.[40]

So it is that, for Newman, the emergence of the individual's initial image of God has its roots in our affective life, in our human
experience. Of course, this initial image must be expanded, deep-
ened and completed 'by means of education, social intercourse,
experience, and literature', and Newman was well aware that individual temperament and circumstances are significant factors in
this regard.

At least initially, the individual experiences God primarily as
'Lawgiver' and 'Judge'. God is He who 'enjoins' and 'enforces'
'what is right and good'. He makes Himself known in a summons, a moral imperative, that is to say, in the call to ethical
praxis. The quality of the soul's response to that call determines,
in no small measure, the subsequent evolution of the nascent relationship between itself and the Deity. Through its submission
to or its refusal of the divine command (which, admittedly, is not
always 'clear and distinct'), the soul sketches, as it were, its own
likeness of the Divinity. One might say, then, that the soul's encounter with God in conscience is as much a question of praxis as
of sentiment. In this sense, Jan Walgrave rightly describes the intimate relationship between the soul and God which conscience
makes possible as 'an absolute religious goal'.[41]

According to Newman, men and women whose minds have absorbed the fundamental lessons of natural religion spontaneously
discern a providential hand guiding 'in mercy or in judgement
the physical and moral system', and even the affairs of individuals.
For Newman, some notion of God's providential 'governance' of
the world and human affairs is basic to natural religion.[42]

Hence, in Newman's vision, the experience of conscience, while it reveals God as a lawgiver, simultaneously reveals Him as One who wills our happiness and has ordered creation accordingly. From the outset then, the individual looks to the divine lawgiver as to a benevolent ruler, who has one's best interests at heart.[43]

It is the individual's instinctive awareness that a benevolent providence intends its good, through the medium of conscience, which accounts for the emergence of the second and third characteristics of natural religion in Newman's scheme, namely, prayer and hope. The former, which encompasses a whole range of activities of worship, serves as the vehicle par excellence for the expression of the latter.[44]

The individual's sense of God's providential goodness is so profound that hope persists even in the face of the individual's failure to honour adequately the moral law he/she perceives within. Indeed, precisely in the critical moment of the confrontation with one's own inadequacy and confusion, hope acquires a new and bolder form. It issues in the 'expectation' that the same providential goodness who draws one on to moral perfection will intervene on one's behalf:

> One of the most important effects of Natural Religion on the mind, in preparation for Revealed, is the anticipation which it creates, that a Revelation will be given.... This presentiment is founded on our sense, on the one hand, of the infinite goodness of God, and, on the other, of our own extreme misery and need – two doctrines which are the primary constituents of Natural Religion.[45]

So it is that the expectation of a revelation, that is to say, of some initiative on the part of the divine, emerges, for Newman, as an 'integral part of Natural Religion'.[46] The naturally religious person is, as it were, on the lookout for God,[47] and ascribes even the rites and ceremonies by means of which he/she seeks to appease the Deity to the latter's revelatory activity.[48]

As far as the rites of paganism were concerned, Newman displayed a remarkable liberty. In the *Apologia*, Newman records his discovery of the Alexandrian Church's view that 'pagan literature, philosophy, and mythology, properly understood, were ... a preparation for the Gospel'[49] (a theme taken up in Vatican II). In *The Arians of the Fourth Century* (1833), he affirmed 'the divinity of traditionary religion', that is to say, what he, following Clement

of Alexandria, described as the 'dispensation of paganism'.[50] 'All
knowledge of religion', he wrote, 'is from [God], and not only
that which the Bible has transmitted to us. There never was a time
when God had not spoken to man, and told him to a certain extent his duty.' By religion Newman meant the living relationship
between the believer and a personal God. Religion is that whole
complex of human actions, including ethical and devotional practice (and eventually the assent of faith), which has as its object a
divine reality.[51] It is with this notion in mind that Newman could
make the remarkable assertion that 'Revelation, properly speaking, is an universal, not a local gift.'[52] In *The Arians*, he speaks of
the 'vague and uncertain family of religious truths, originally
from God', which permeate the 'Dispensation of Paganism'[53] (also
a conciliar theme).

In an excellent study of Newman's views on the 'economy of
salvation', Erwin Ender has pointed out that Newman did not
simply copy the Alexandrian doctrine but instead adapted it in
the light of his own sensitivity to the demands of concrete history. Hence, Newman does not pay much attention to the doctrine of the Logos, which had served the Fathers in accounting
for the wisdom of Greek philosophy, but turns instead to the
'natural religion' of paganism since this was a more widespread
phenomenon, more accessible to the great mass of non-
Christians.[54] Newman, the empiricist, is not given to abstract
speculation, even if it has patristic sanction. He prefers to concentrate on the concrete working out of the economy of salvation
in history.

In this respect, he bears witness to the suggestion made above
that inclusivism is perhaps best characterized as a theology of religions which focuses on the mediation of salvation, that is to say,
on the form in which God's universal salvific will is made real for
historical human beings. This attention to concrete forms is reflected in Newman's conviction that God uses the rites and customs of pagan religions to realize His salvific will. In *The Idea of
a University*, he writes as follows:

> He [God] introduces Himself, He all but concurs, according to
> His good pleasure, and in His selected season, in the issues of un-
> belief, superstition, and false worship, and He changes the char-
> acter of acts by His overruling operation. He condescends, though
> He gives no sanction, to the altars and shrines of imposture, and
> He makes His own fiat the substitute for its sorceries. He speaks
> amid the incantations of Balaam, raises Samuel's spirit in the

witch's cavern, prophesies of the Messiah by the tongue of the Sibyl ... and baptizes by the hand of the misbeliever.[55]

As I have already indicated, the suggestion that God might indeed employ non-Christian forms of religious practice and association to work His salvific will is a distinctly post-conciliar idea. While we cannot take this passage as proof that Newman thought in these terms (though Ender apparently does), we must at least acknowledge that his reflections are not incompatible with this view. In this regard, it is interesting to note that the co-editor of the series within which Newman's *Arians of the Fourth Century* appeared objected to Newman's defence of the principle that all religion comes from God.[56]

Newman's conviction that God works through 'various Economies or Dispensations' to achieve His (one) salvific will apparently led him to raise a possibility which Vatican II never considered, namely, that the mediation of the Church might not be essential for the salvation of every man and woman. The Second Vatican Council appears to teach that the Church is always at least implicated in the salvific process realized in Christ (by virtue of its role as the 'universal sacrament of salvation', which 'represents' Christ's redemptive work, especially in the Eucharist).[57] Newman, however, as early as 1832 observes that God 'can sustain our immortality without the Christian sacraments as He sustained Abraham and the other saints of old time'.[58] And, on another occasion, he reflected, 'As just men existed before Christ came, why not at a distance from the Church? For what the former is of time, so just men among the heathen is of space.'[59] In a most remarkable declaration, he even goes so far as to reflect that 'it does not follow, because there is no Church but one, which has the Evangelical gifts and privileges to bestow, that therefore no one can be saved without the intervention of that one Church'.[60]

Of course, we must not push this too far. Newman was no pluralist. His theology of religions is radically incarnational. 'All the providences of God centre' in Christ, he wrote in the *Grammar*.[61] His salvific work 'is the sole Meritorious Cause, the sole Source of spiritual blessing to our guilty race',[62] and the Church, especially via its sacramental life, exists to render that blessing accessible to humanity.[63] As Ian Ker has pointed out, Newman did not hesitate to ally himself, as a Catholic, with the view of Duns Scotus, against Thomas Aquinas, that the Incarnation would have found place even if humanity had never sinned.[64] The 'various economies of salvation' find their focus in the Christ-event. The Incarnation constitutes the unifying principle of salvation history in all its diversity.[65] Hence, Newman is quite insistent that faith in Christ and a share in the Church's life are the 'ordinary' and most reliable way to salvation.[66]

Of course, Newman's thought on these matters was not well developed and what he does say was clearly not elaborated in view of the concerns of the contemporary theology of religions. Nevertheless, his reflections on the possible salvific utility, as it were, of non-Christian religious practices, his willingness to apply the term 'revelation' to non-Christian religious truth, and his preparedness to reduce the visible Church's instrumental role in the economy of salvation should give us pause for thought. If as convinced an inclusivist as Newman can entertain these notions, might not the official Church do the same?

The Character of the God of Conversion (Pluralism, Alterity and the Claim of Natural Religion)

It is immediately evident that Newman was not a pluralist. The primary incompatibility between pluralism and Newman is, not surprisingly, the notion of 'revelation'. The pluralist critique of inclusivism goes far beyond the question of the strategy to be adopted in interreligious dialogue. What is at stake is the nature and purpose of revelation and, by extension, the nature and will of the God who reveals.

I have already mentioned the pluralist insistence that the Transcendent Reality (what Hick calls the 'Real'[67] and Christians call God, the Father of Jesus Christ) is ultimately a Mystery, the Unutterable who can only be approached by a radical *via negativa*.[68] I have also spoken of the pluralist aversion to the notion that a distinctive revelation might have been given to one (so-called 'privileged') people or age. Both these characteristics of the pluralist theology of religions would have made it repugnant to Newman. Indeed, Newman would certainly have seen in pluralism the progeny of that Liberalism he had dedicated his entire life to combating. In this regard, one cannot but be struck by the remarkable parallelism between the description of pluralism recently offered by the British theologian, Lesslie Newbigin, and Newman's depiction of nineteenth-century Liberalism (a parallel made all the more remarkable by the fact that Newbigin displays no familiarity with Newman). Newbigin describes pluralism as follows:

> Religious pluralism ... is the belief that the differences between the religions are not a matter of truth and falsehood, but of different perceptions of the one truth; that to speak of religious beliefs as true or false is inadmissible. Religious belief is a private matter. Each of us is entitled to have – as we say – a faith of our own. This is religious pluralism, and it is a widely held opinion in contemporary British society.[69]

On the occasion of his elevation as Cardinal (1879), Newman described Liberalism as follows:

> Liberalism in religion is the doctrine that there is no positive truth in religion, but that one creed is as good as another, and this is the teaching which is gaining substance and force daily. It is inconsistent with any recognition of any religion as *true*. It teaches that all are to be tolerated, for all are matters of opinion.[70]

Lee H. Yearley has attempted to outline the foundational principles of the Liberalism Newman resisted. One of the most significant of these is the view of revelation as 'an ever-present situation', the manifestation of an 'omnipresent divine reality' in 'humanity's historical experience'.[71] In Newman's words, the Liberals regarded revelation as 'a single, entire, solitary act'.[72] Liberalism culminated in the insistence that 'the divine is most adequately grasped, not by an attachment to a single revelation, but by a view that looks through specific revelations and includes all the existing, varying, and limiting manifestations of the sacred'.[73]

According to the Liberals, particular historical events and particular religious leaders acquire religious significance in the measure that they manifest the ever-present divine. Newman saw Liberalism as resolving Christ into 'a moral Manifestation of God', and the Atonement as no more than a 'mark and pledge of God's love'.[74]

This portrayal of Liberalism is remarkably coincident with our earlier description of contemporary pluralist theology. There, too, 'God is manifest differently through the various scriptures, prophets and sages of the religions'. There, too, only a collaborative effort among the world's religious traditions can provide for an acceptable image of God. There, too, revelation is a universally accessible religious experience. There, too, Jesus is valued for his moral authority and his significance as an expression of divine love.[75]

Clearly, Newman would have regarded contemporary pluralist theology just as he regarded nineteenth-century Liberalism, namely, as a 'great mischief' which undermines the foundations (and ultimately the possibility) of Christian faith.[76]

Newman's celebrated claim that there is no medium between atheism and Catholicity hinged on his equally celebrated conviction that religious life can only be sustained if it is rooted in a revelatory tradition which is possessed of its own authority. He regarded Liberalism as 'a half-way house tending towards atheism' precisely because Liberalism was inspired by 'the anti-dogmatic principle', that is to say, by the insistence that every religious claim be completely comprehensible in human terms (epistemological, psychological, sociological and so forth). What Liberalism sought, and what Newman could not countenance, was religion within the limits of reason alone.[77]

The pluralist theology of religions is certainly characterized by a Liberal determination to eliminate all those doctrinal claims which are not compatible with its own first principles, the most prominent of these being the refusal of a particular historical revelation. Hence, pluralist theologians rightly portray their theology of religions as the culmination of an evolutive process, a progressive movement through four distinctive stages: from *ecclesiocentrism* (where the Church occupies the central place), to *Christocentrism* (where Christ is regarded as central), to *theocentrism* (where the Transcendent as such is central), to *soteriocentrism*. The latter, as we have said, is characterized by the determination to focus not on doctrinal or 'theo-logical' issues but on the goal of salvation.[78]

Newman's linking of Liberalism and atheism would seem to be supported as well by the fact that theologians sympathetic to the pluralist viewpoint, such as the Cambridge theologian, Don Cupitt, have questioned whether it is necessary to postulate a transcendent Reality behind human religious constructs. After all, what is at stake is not the transcendent Real, which is ultimately Unknown and unknowable, but the spiritual and/or soterio-centric effectiveness of the religions themselves. And that does not appear to be dependent on the nature of the elusive deity to whom these traditions refer.[79]

It is characteristic of natural religion that it provides its adherents with a well-defined deity, a deity whose features are even, so to speak, alarmingly distinctive. The God of natural religion is a merciful judge, a demanding benefactor, the source of the moral law and of human hope, an unrelenting taskmaster who seeks to alleviate the burdens He imposes on us. In *The Arians*, Newman says of natural religion that it teaches us 'the doctrines of the power and presence of an invisible God, of His moral law and governance, of the obligation of duty, and the certainty of a just judgement, and of reward and punishment, as eventually dispensed to individuals'.[80] In the *Grammar*, he describes the God of natural religion as 'a Supreme Governor, a Judge, holy, just, powerful, all-seeing, [and] retributive'.[81]

The God of natural religion is the God who calls us out of ourselves to serve Him and our fellows. He is the God of conversion. And He is the God of revelation or, more accurately, the God from whom a distinctive, liberating revelation is to be expected.

It is one of the great paradoxes of pluralist theology that, in its attempt to do justice to the true nature of the Transcendent, by liberating it from the constraints of particular revelatory claims, it deprives it of all substance. The Absolute or the Real so dear to pluralists is ultimately a God with no face, only a multitude of names. Karl Barth has described this deity as 'the unsubstantial, unprofitable, and fundamentally very tedious magnitude known as transcendence'.

> It is characteristic of this transcendence [Barth continues,] that it neither has a specific will, nor accomplishes a specific act, nor speaks a specific word, nor exercises specific power and authority. It can neither bind man effectively nor liberate him. It can neither justify nor satisfy him. It cannot be for his life either a clear meaning or a distinct purpose.[82]

The pluralist theology of religions seems to self-destruct as far as the postmodern theme of 'otherness' is concerned. By this I mean that it moves from the declared aim of acknowledging alterity to a theological programme which effectively obliterates any and all claims to a distinctive religious truth. Is not pluralism, at least as far as its tendency to level out doctrinal differences is concerned, reminiscent of what David Tracy (quoting Simone de Beauvoir) has described as the 'perfect ideology for the modern bourgeois mind', namely, 'a passive response to more and more possibilities, none of which shall ever be practised'?[83]

The Anthropology of Conversion (Inclusivism, Relativity and the Challenge of Natural Religion)

In his consideration of the relationship between 'natural' and 'revealed' religion, Newman mixes historical analysis and what would now be described as a 'phenomenological' investigation of his own personal experience. Moreover, he never clearly distinguishes these. As Lee H. Yearley has pointed out, Newman's reflections on the history of religions evidence a Victorian provincialism, and his endeavour to establish an historical or 'chronological' connection between natural and revealed religion involves him in serious theological and historical problems.[84]

However, as Yearley himself acknowledges, these problems do not detract from Newman's real achievement. Newman's concern was not the historical progress of religion (though he was, of course, intrigued by this problematic) but the religious progress of concrete, historical individuals, most of whom had been exposed to Christianity from infancy and many of whom had rejected it, or threatened to reject it, as untenable. Newman's aim was to demonstrate, as it were, that the human person is naturally religious and that Christianity is the fulfilment of, the only adequate answer to, our religious aspirations.

'In Christians themselves', Newman writes, natural religion 'cannot really be separated from their Christianity'.[85]

The Christian's position vis-à-vis the conscientious adherents of natural religion is then not unlike that of St Paul vis-à-vis the Athenians in Acts 17.23 – subject to the same God and the same law but sure in the knowledge of Him 'whom they worship as unknown'.

However, the Christian's privileged position by no means implies a lessening of the moral or religious burden. On the contrary, 'Revelation puts us on a trial which exists but obscurely in Natural Religion; the trial of being obedient for obedience-sake, or on Faith.'[86]

Mere membership of a revealed religion does not guarantee our salvation. For Newman, the superstitious pagan, who views all that he/she sees as the revelation of the divine will – and more often than not, the divine anger – is preferable to the self-sufficient and self-wise Christian who has banished religion to the periphery of his or her existence.[87]

Dark and fierce though it may often be (and Newman was convinced that natural religion 'almost invariably [had] worn its dark side outwards'[88]), natural religion is 'man's truest and best religion, before the Gospel shines on him'.[89] Moreover, 'they who are not superstitious without the Gospel, will not be religious with it'.[90] The pagan, with his interest in auguries and omens, and his mythical reading of history, is intent on God, even though (or precisely because) he has come to know Him, above all, under the category of 'retributive justice'. In the final analysis, Newman's concern is neither paganism's fierceness nor its manifest poly-theism, though he is stern in his denouncement of both. His real concern – and it is this which establishes his analysis as, in the first place, a phenomenological one – is the religious state of mind, born of attention to those 'primary mental experiences' which ground all religious practice and profession and which, Newman insisted, were the common property of humanity.[91]

Summary Conclusion: Experience, Alterity and Relativity in Newman's Theology of Religions

Newman's interest in the religious experience of the 'naturally' re-ligious man or woman dovetails neatly with the postmodern in-sistence that all religious claims be tested in the crucible of personal experience. Moreover, the attention Newman accords to the element of experience compensates for the neglect of this theme in the inclusivist approach.

The God of natural religion is defined primarily in terms of the call to conversion. The God who makes His presence felt in the experience of the 'naturally' religious man and woman is the Just Benefactor who summons us beyond ourselves to ever more pro-found devotional and ethical praxis. Newman's discussion of this element of natural religion can serve as a corrective to pluralism's reluctance to define the Transcendent 'Real' in any meaningful fashion, a reluctance which puts paid to pluralism's claim to take other religions seriously in their 'otherness'. Newman's acknow-ledgement of the distinctly 'religious' content of human religious constructs would seem to do non-Christian traditions more jus-tice than either pluralism or traditional Catholic inclusivism.

Finally, the response given to the call to conversion at the heart of natural religion is determinative of our future religious progress. Indeed, the possibility of faith in a particular revelation is dependent on that more fundamental religious disposition which is within the reach of everyone. Newman's discussion of this element of natural religion points up the fact that mere pos-session of a distinct divine revelation means nothing in and of it-self. Every particular religious tradition, including Christianity, can, in a sense, be measured against the fundamental religious de-mand for conversion. Moreover, every religion which places a premium on conversion has a claim on us and can serve as a chal-

lenge to us. This insight encourages a spirit of humility with respect to one's own tradition and a recognition that what is most
basic to 'religion' is universal. It is, so to speak, the common
property of humanity.

Accordingly, as my title indicates, the call to conversion need
not be seen as the concern of professed Christians alone. Instead,
it might be portrayed as an anthropological reality, as a dimension
of our humanity. As such, it can serve as a theme around which
all the world's religions can unite. In my view, Newman's treatment of this element is one of the most timely aspects of his
theology of religions, and one which gives him a voice in the
contemporary debate.

Notes

1. Pope Paul VI described Newman as in a unique sense the theologian of the Second Vatican Council ('the invisible *peritus*'), and also of the present time. See John Coulson, 'Newman's Hour: The Significance of Newman's Thought and its Application Today', *Heythrop Journal* 22 (1981) 394. I have reflected on Newman's theological methodology in 'Newman on the Practice of Theology', *Louvain Studies* 14 (1989) 260–84.

2. For an assessment of Newman's relationship to the Second Vatican Council, written shortly after its completion, see B. C. Butler, 'Newman and the Second Vatican Council', in *The Rediscovery of Newman: An Oxford Symposium*, ed. J. Coulson, A. M. Allchin (London: SPCK, 1967) 233–46. Butler acknowledges (p. 245) that Newman's influence on the Council 'cannot be found to have been deep or determinative', but he does venture that the Council marked a turning of the 'tide', and a 'first, immensely important step . . . towards the vindication of all the main theological, religious, and cultural positions' of Newman. This view is endorsed by Stephen Dessain, *Newman's Spiritual Themes* (Dublin: Veritas, 1977) 31. In his 'Tides and Twilight: Newman Since Vatican II', in *Newman after a Hundred Years*, ed. Ian Ker, Alan G. Hill (Oxford: Clarendon, 1990) 447–64, Nicholas Lash suggests that the Council promoted a theological climate which encouraged a reevaluation of Newman's insights and significance. In this respect, he comments (p. 450) that 'it may be more fruitful to consider the council's influence on Newman's accessibility to the Catholic imagination than to pursue the quest for traces of Newman's (exceedingly) limited influence upon the council'. For a reflection on Newman's significance for the contemporary Church, see Ian Ker, 'Newman and the Postconciliar Church', in *Newman Today*, ed. S. J. Jaki (San Francisco: Ignatius Press, 1989) 121–41; 'Newman and the "Orphans of Vatican II"', *Louvain Studies* 15 (1990) 119–35. Ker, 'Newman and the Postconciliar Church', 121 observes that 'Vatican II upheld and vindicated those controversial positions that [Newman] espoused in his own time, and so often at his own personal cost.'

3. See, for example, R. J. Bernstein, *Beyond Objectivism and Relativism: Science, Hermeneutics, and Praxis* (Oxford, 1983) 1–20.

4. See David Tracy, *Dialogue with the Other: The Inter-Religious Dialogue*, Louvain Theological and Pastoral Monographs, 1 (Louvain: Peeters, 1990).

5. On Newman's empiricism, see J. M. Cameron, 'Newman and the Empiricist Tradition', in *The Rediscovery of Newman: An Oxford Symposium*, 82; 'Newman and Locke: A Note on Some Themes in "An Essay In Aid Of A Grammar Of Assent"', *Newman Studien*, ed. H. Fries, W. Becker (Heroldsberg bei Nürnberg: Glock und Lutz, 1974) 9: 200.

6. Edward Schillebeeckx is of the opinion that the term 'unique' is no longer serviceable as far as the discussion of Christianity's specificity is concerned, since all religions are unique as far as their own historical identity is concerned. He proposes, therefore, that we speak of the 'definitive and universal significance' of Christianity. By 'definitive' Schillebeeckx means that, 'according to the Christian confession of faith, God, in Jesus Christ, has made clear His ultimate intentions with regard to humanity'. By 'universal' he means that 'the evangelical message is directed to all people and can be accepted as meaningful by all people, and that this message embraces all significant dimensions of human existence'. We would accept this terminological refinement. It does not, however, resolve the issue of the normative character of Christianity with respect to the world's other religious traditions. See Edward Schillebeeckx, 'Identiteit, eigenheid en universaliteit van Gods heil in Jezus', *Tijdschrift voor Theologie* 34 (1990) 260–1. See also Edward Schillebeeckx, 'The Religious and the Human Ecumene', *The Future of Liberation Theology: Essays in Honor of Gustavo Gutiérrez*, ed. M. E. Ellis, O. Maduro (Maryknoll, N.Y.: Orbis, 1989) 32–45.

7. Paul F. Knitter, 'Preface' to *The Myth of Christian Uniqueness*, ed. J. Hick, P. Knitter (Maryknoll, N.Y.: Orbis, 1988) vii.

8. Langdon Gilkey, 'Plurality and its Theological Implications', *The Myth of Christian Uniqueness*, 37. Knitter speaks of a 'possible' parity. See Paul Knitter, 'Key Questions for a Theology of Religions', *Horizons* 17 (1990) 93.

9. *The Myth of Christian Uniqueness*, ed. J. Hick, P. Knitter (Maryknoll, N.Y.: Orbis, 1988).

10. Paul F. Knitter, 'Preface' to *The Myth of Christian Uniqueness*, viii; see also Knitter's 'The Pluralist Move and its Critics', *The Drew Gateway* 58 (1988) 4–10. For a discussion of three 'classical' tendencies, see A. Kreiner, 'Die Erfahrung religiöser Vielfalt', in *Religiöse Erfahrung und theologische Reflexion. Festschrift für Heinrich Döring*, ed. A. Kreiner, P. Schmidt-Leukel (Paderborn, 1993) 323–35. K. Yandell observes that the pluralist school itself is characterized by a plurality of approaches. See his 'Some Varieties of Religious Pluralism', in *Inter-Religious Models and Criteria*, ed. J. Kellenberger (London: Macmillan, 1993) 187–211.

11. Chester Gillis, *Pluralism: A New Paradigm for Theology*, Louvain Theological and Pastoral Monographs, 12 (Louvain: Peeters, 1993) 171.

12. John Hick borrows this term from the work of Karl Jaspers, who spoke of the 'Achsenzeit', to describe the period between 800 and 200 BC, when an evolution 'from archaic religion to the religions of salvation or liberation' took place. See John Hick, *An Interpretation of Religion: Human Responses to the Transcendent* (London: Macmillan, 1989) 29–33.

13. See, for example, Hick, *An Interpretation of Religion*, 14: 'The infinite Real, in itself beyond the scope of other than purely formal concepts, is differently conceived, experienced and responded to from within the different cultural ways of being human.' See also John Hick, *The Metaphor of God Incarnate* (London: SCM, 1993) 38–9: '[Religious experiences] are thus jointly products of the universal presence of the ultimately Real, of the special circumstances that cause individuals at particular moments to be open to that reality, and of the concepts and images in terms of which their conscious experience is constructed.'

14. Hick, *An Interpretation of Religion*, 154.

15. *Ibid.*

16. Gillis, *Pluralism: A New Paradigm for Theology*, 177–80. See John Hick, 'An Inspiration Christology for a Religiously Plural World', *Encountering Jesus: A Debate on Christology* (Atlanta: John Knox Press, 1988) 32–3 where Hick explains that 'the Real, *an sich*, is not the object of a cult. It is the ultimate reality that we postulate as the ground of the different forms of religious experience and thought insofar as these are more than human projections.'

17. Hick, *Metaphor of God Incarnate*, 104, 13, 98.

18. Hick, *Metaphor of God Incarnate*, 160.

19. Regarding the polar character of religious truth, see, for example, Raimundo Panikkar,

'The Jordan, the Tiber and the Ganges: Three Kairological Moments of Christic Self-Consciousness', *The Myth of Christian Uniqueness*, ed. J. Hick, P. Knitter (Maryknoll, N.Y.: Orbis, 1988) 102, 103, 110; Paul Knitter, *No Other Name? A Critical Survey of Christian Attitudes Toward the World Religions* (Maryknoll, N.Y.: Orbis, 1985) 220. In an article which appeared in 1990, 'Interreligious Dialogue: What? Why? How?', *Death or Dialogue? From the Age of Monologue to the Age of Dialogue* (London: SCM, 1990) 20–1, Knitter acknowledges that the differences among the world's religions are greater than he had previously suggested. In this context, one must take the existing situation of plurality as the point of departure 'before we can ever contemplate, much less realize, their possible unity or oneness'.

20. Regarding the theme of 'crossing-over', see Knitter, *No Other Name?*, 53, 209, 210, 212, 213.

21. S. Mark Heim, *Salvations: Truth and Difference in Religion* (Maryknoll, N.Y.: Orbis, 1995) 129.

22. Hick, *An Interpretation of Religion*, 12, 14. See also John Hick, 'Interpretation and Reinterpretation in Religion', *The Making and Remaking of Christian Doctrine: Essays in Honour of Maurice Wiles*, ed. S. Coakley, D. A. Pailin (Oxford: Clarendon, 1993) 69: 'For we see taking place within each of the great traditions, and taking place to more or less the same extent, the salvific transformation of human life, individually and corporately, from destructive self-centredness to a new orientation centred in the divine Reality.'

23. Paul Knitter's recent theology has tended to concentrate on the soteriocentric approach to interreligious dialogue. See his 'Toward a Liberation Theology of Religions', *The Myth of Christian Uniqueness*, 178–200; 'A Liberation-Centered Theology of Religions', *The Drew Gateway* 58 (1988) 22–9. See also his *One Earth Many Religions: Multifaith Dialogue and Global Responsibility* (Maryknoll, N.Y.: Orbis, 1995) 36 where Knitter describes *soteria* as 'human and ecological well-being'.

24. Paul Knitter, Preface to *The Myth of Christian Uniqueness*, viii. In addition to these two concerns, pluralist theologians insist that believers must give priority to the growing cry for justice and liberation which rises up from the world's oppressed.

25. *Ibid.*, ix. The authors who contributed to *The Myth of Christian Uniqueness* were invited 'to formulate their views on why they felt the contemporary context was pressing Christians toward a new pluralist approach toward other religions'.

26. For an extensive discussion of the evolution of the teaching, 'extra ecclesiam nulla salus', see Francis A. Sullivan, *Salvation Outside the Church?* (New York: Paulist, 1992).

27. *Nostra Aetate*, no. 2. All references to conciliar documents will be taken from *Decrees of the Ecumenical Councils*, 2 vols, ed. N. P. Tanner (London: Sheed & Ward; Washington: Georgetown University Press, 1990).

28. See *Lumen Gentium*, nos 1, 9, 48; *Ad Gentes*, no. 1; *Gaudium et Spes*, no. 45.

29. See *Nostra Aetate*, no. 1.

30. See *Nostra Aetate*, no. 2.

31. Clearly, Judaism constitutes a case apart. Heinz Robert Schlette, however, observes that, 'from the point of view of the history of salvation and of the related concept of special revelation, it is regrettable that in the end the Council gave its views on the Jewish religion, and in particular on anti-Semitism, within the framework of [the *Declaration on the Church's Relation to Non-Christian Religions*] and under the title it bears'. See H. R. Schlette, *Encyclopedia of Theology: A Concise Sacramentum Mundi*, ed. Karl Rahner (London: Burns & Oates, 1975), s.v. 'Religion; III. Theology of Religions', 1396–7.

32. *Ibid.* There is, however, obvious movement in Catholic theology in this regard. In a statement issued in 1991, entitled *Dialogue and Proclamation*, the Vatican Council for Interreligious Dialogue and the Congregation for the Evangelization of Peoples claimed that Vatican II 'has openly acknowledged the presence of positive values not only in the religious life of individual believers of other religious traditions, but also in the religious traditions to which they belong. It attributed these values to the active presence of God through his Word, pointing also to the universal action of the Spirit'.

'These elements', the statement continues, 'still play a providential role in the divine economy of salvation' (no. 17). While insisting that there is 'but one plan of salvation for humankind, with its centre in Jesus Christ' (no. 28), who constitutes its 'final fulfilment' (no. 19), the statement does acknowledge that 'concretely, it will be in the sincere practice of what is good in their own religious traditions and by following the dictates of their conscience that the members of other religions respond positively to God's invitation and receive salvation in Jesus Christ, even while they do not recognize or acknowledge him as their saviour' (no. 29). See the text of 'Dialogue and Proclamation: Reflections and Orientations on Interreligious Dialogue and the Proclamation of the Gospel of Jesus Christ', in *Redemption and Dialogue: Reading 'Redemptoris Missio' and 'Dialogue and Proclamation'*, ed. W. R. Burrows (New York: Orbis, 1993) 93–118. See the remarks on the document by Jacques Dupuis, 'A Theological Commentary: Dialogue and Proclamation', in *Redemption and Dialogue*, 119–58, especially 137 where Dupuis reflects on the claim that non-Christians are saved – by Jesus Christ – in 'the sincere practice of what is good in their religious traditions' (no. 29). Dupuis observes that this 'is a weighty statement, not found before in official documents of the central teaching authority, and whose theological import must not be underestimated. It means, in effect, that the members of other religions are not saved by Christ in spite of, or beside, their own tradition, but in it and in some mysterious way, "known to God", through it. If further elaborated theologically, this statement would be seen to imply some hidden presence – no matter how imperfect – of the mystery of Jesus Christ in these religious traditions in which salvation reaches their adherents.'

33. For a survey of the Catholic theology of religions since Vatican II, see Paul Knitter, *No Other Name? A Critical Survey of Christian Attitudes Toward the World Religions* (Maryknoll, N.Y.: Orbis, 1985) 120–44. For a discussion of the notion that the world's religions constitute the 'ordinary' way to salvation while Christianity constitutes the 'extraordinary' way (although it remains the preferred way), see Hans Küng, 'The World Religions in God's Plan of Salvation', *Christian Revelation and World Religions*, ed. Joseph Neuner (London: Burns & Oates, 1967) 51–3, and Heinz Robert Schlette, *Towards a Theology of Religions* (London: Burns & Oates, 1966) 80–1. See Knitter, *No Other Name?*, 127.

34. As examples of these three approaches, one thinks of Karl Rahner, Hans Küng and Gavin D'Costa respectively. See, for example, Karl Rahner, 'Christianity and the Non-Christian Religions', *Theological Investigations*, vol. 5 (Baltimore: Helicon, 1966) 115–34; Hans Küng, 'The World Religions in God's Plan of Salvation', *Christian Revelation and World Religions*, ed. J. Neuner (London: Burns & Oates, 1967) 25–66; Gavin D'Costa, 'Towards a Trinitarian Theology of Religions', *A Universal Faith? Peoples, Cultures, Religions and the Christ*, ed. C. Cornille, V. Neckebrouck (Louvain: Peeters, 1992) 139–54. The work of process theologians, such as John Cobb, would appear to belong to the third category. See, for example, John Cobb, *Christ in a Pluralistic World* (Philadelphia: Westminster, 1975).

35. I have discussed Newman's understanding of conscience at length in my 'Newman's Experience of God: An Interpretive Model', *Bijdragen* 48 (1987) 444–64. See also ' "Numquam minus solus quam cum solus": Newman's First Conversion – Its Significance for His Life and Thought', *Downside Review* 103 (1985) 99–116; 'Newman's Oriel Experience: Its Significance for His Life and Thought', *Bijdragen* 47 (1986) 200–21; *Clear Heads and Holy Hearts: The Religious and Theological Ideal of John Henry Newman*, Louvain Theological and Pastoral Monographs, 7 (Louvain: Peeters, 1991) 36–41.

36. All references to Newman's works will employ the now standard abbreviations provided in volume 11 of *The Letters and Diaries of John Henry Newman*, ed. C. S. Dessain (London: Oxford University Press, 1961). References to works published during Newman's lifetime are to the uniform edition, which was published by Longmans, Green & Co. of London between 1868 and 1881. All references to Newman's *Essay on Development* will be to the revised 1878 edition. The abbreviation *PN* refers to *The*

Philosophical Notebook of John Henry Newman. ed. Edward Sillem, 2 vols (Louvain: Nauwelaerts, 1969–1970). See *PN*, 2: 33–4. See also 2: 35–7, 43–5, 47, 59, 83; *Apo.*, 4, 198.

37. *PN*, 2: 49, 37, 43, 99; *GA*, 105; *PS*, 5: 318. See also *PN*, 2: 31 n. 2 where the editor indicates that Newman does not mean by feeling a 'sensible feeling, but what we ordinarily call a "feeling" of conscience'. An appropriate term would seem to be 'sentiment'. See *PN*, 2: 59–60; *PS*, 7: 199–200.

38. *PN*, 2: 49. *GA*, 105. See also *GA*, 107–10.

39. *GA*, 105–10, 113, 389–90; *PN*, 2: 53; *Call.*, 174; *PS*, 2: 18; *LD*, 19: 128, 247; 29: 14; 21: 395–96; 24: 275.

40. *GA*, 109–10; *Call.*, 174; *US*, 18–19; *LD*, 24: 275.

41. Jan Hendrik Walgrave, 'Newman vandaag', *Periodieke uitgave van het Geert Groote Genootschap*, 698 ('s Hertogenbosch, 1957) 25.

42. *GA*, 118, 117, 402. See also *PS*, 3: 114–15.

43. See *GA*, 114. Note that on p. 82 of *GA*, Newman places the 'thought' of 'Divine Goodness' before the thought of 'future reward' or 'eternal life' as objects of real assent.

44. *GA*, 403, 401.

45. *GA*, 422–23. See also *GA*, 429; *US*, 21; *Mix.*, 277–79.

46. *GA*, 404–05, 423.

47. *OS*, 66–8; *Mix.*, 276–79; *DA*, 296; *US*, 239–40; *PS*, 2: 17–19.

48. *GA*, 404, 417–18.

49. *Apo.*, 36.

50. *Ari.*, 79, 81. See Erwin Ender, 'Heilsökonomie und Rechtfertigung: Zur Heilsfrage im Leben und Denken Newmans', *Newman Studien*, ed. H. Fries, W. Becker (Heroldsberg bei Nürnberg: Glock und Lutz, 1978) 10: 164 n. 32. As E. Ender points out, 'Um den bedeutenden Unterschied deutlicher hervorzuheben, der trotz vieler Gemeinsamkeiten zwischen der natürlichen und der geoffenbarten Religion grundsätzlich besteht, spricht Newman später in der Via Media nicht mehr einfach von der "Divinity of Paganism", sondern von der "doctrine ... of the indirectly divine character of Paganism".' (See *VM*, 1: 248.) 'Demgegenüber steht "the exclusive divinity of the Mosaic theology" ' (*US*, 164).

51. See, in this regard, *GA*, 55, 98–102, 98, 119.

52. *Ari.*, 79–80.

53. *Ari.*, 80–2. See also *Ess.*, 2: 231–2, where Newman speaks of the 'seeds of truth' in 'the philosophies and religions of men ... though they are not directly divine'. See Ker, 'Newman and the Postconciliar Church', 124 where he points out that Newman's acknowledgement of elements of truth in paganism led him 'to what was then the radical conclusion that the christian apologist or missionary should, "after St. Paul's manner, seek some points in the existing superstitions as the basis of his own instructions, instead of indiscriminately condemning and discarding the whole assemblage of heathen opinions and practices", thus "recovering and purifying, rather than reversing the essential principles of their belief" '. See Newman, *Ari.*, 80–1, 84. Compare Newman's remarks in this regard and Vatican II's *Decree on the Missionary Activity of the Church, Ad Gentes*, no. 9: 'Whatever truth and grace are already to be found among peoples – a secret presence of God, so to speak – it [missionary activity] frees from evil infections and restores to Christ their source ... accordingly, whatever good is found to be sown in the minds and hearts of human beings or in the particular rites and cultures of peoples, not only does not perish but is healed, elevated and perfected, to the glory of God, the confusion of the devil and the happiness of humankind.'

54. See n. 48; Ender, 'Heilsökonomie und Rechtfertigung', 155.

55. *Idea*, 65–6; *Ari..*, 82. See Ender, 'Heilsökonomie und Rechtfertigung', 156.

56. Ian Ker, *John Henry Newman: A Biography* (Oxford: Oxford University Press, 1988) 52.

57. With regard to this question, see Sullivan, *Salvation Outside the Church?*

58. *PS*, 1: 275.

59. *SN*, 328. Ender, 'Heilsökonomie und Rechtfertigung', 167 nn. 74, 75 notes that

Newman makes a distinction between the 'ordinary' and the 'extraordinary' way of salvation. The sacraments constitute the former. He describes the extraordinary way, especially in the light of Christ's Incarnation, as an 'uncovenanted mercy'. See *PS*, 1: 275; *Idea*, 183; *SD*, 366.

60. *Diff.*, 2: 335.
61. *GA*, 57.
62. *PS*, 2: 304.
63. See on this theme Ian Ker, *Healing the Wound of Humanity: The Spirituality of John Henry Newman* (London: Darton, Longman & Todd, 1993) 60–7; see also Ender, 'Heilsökonomie und Rechtfertigung', 160–1.
64. Ian Ker, *Newman on Being a Christian* (Notre Dame: University of Notre Dame Press, 1990) 41–2; see also Ian Ker, *Healing the Wound of Humanity*, 27–8. See John Henry Newman, *Discourses to Mixed Congregations*, 321–2, 358.
65. See Ender, 'Heilsökonomie und Rechtfertigung', 158–9.
66. See Ender, 'Heilsökonomie und Rechtfertigung', 160–3; see n. 64 above. Newman insists that the Roman Catholic Church is the only 'religious body ... in which is salvation' (see *Letters and Diaries*, 26: 364; 30: 33–4.) However, he also insists that the teaching, 'extra ecclesiam nulla salus', did not apply to people in invincible ignorance – a principle which Rome was compelled to defend as late as the mid twentieth century (against the claims of the American Jesuit, Leonard Feeney). See *Letters and Diaries*, 25: 71. See Ker, *Newman: A Biography*, 680–1.
67. See n. 13 above.
68. For a critical reflection on the legitimacy of the pluralist appeal to the ineffable character of God, see Keith Ward, 'Divine Ineffability', in *God, Truth and Reality: Essays in Honour of John Hick*, ed. Arvind Sharma (New York: St Martin's Press, 1993) 210–20, especially 211–12, 215.
69. Lesslie Newbigin, *The Gospel in a Pluralist Society* (Grand Rapids, Michigan: W. B. Eerdmans; Geneva: WCC Publications, 1989) 14.
70. *Campaign*, 393. In his *Essay on Development*, Newman described Liberalism in these terms:

> That truth and falsehood in religion are but matter of opinion ...; that there is no truth; that we are not more acceptable to God by believing this than by believing that; that no one is answerable for his opinions; that they are a matter of necessity or accident; that it is enough if we sincerely hold what we profess ...; that we may safely trust to ourselves in matters of faith – this is the principle of philosophies and heresies. ...

See *Dev.*, 357–8; see also *Apo.*, 294–5.
71. Lee H. Yearley, *The Ideas of Newman: Christianity and Human Religiosity* (University Park, Pa.: The Pennsylvania State University Press 1978) 110–11, 112. I have discussed other elements of Yearley's discussion and provided a critique of his views in my ' "One momentous doctrine which enters into my reasoning": The Unitive Function of Newman's Doctrine of Providence', *Downside Review* 108 (1990) 264–9. Yearley also characterizes Liberalism as advocating that people 'go beyond any particular revelation and seek the underlying essence of all revelations'. Contemporary pluralists are very cautious as far as the notion of a common essence of religion is concerned. See, for example, Paul Knitter, 'Interreligious Dialogue: What? Why? How?', *Death or Dialogue? From the Age of Monologue to the Age of Dialogue* (London: SCM, 1990) 20–1.
72. *Ess.*, 2: 213–14.
73. *Ibid.*, 113. The quotation is taken from Newman's *Apologia*, p. 260. Yearley points out that Newman saw Milman's *History of Christianity* as an example of the Liberal tendency. See Newman, *Ess.*, 2: 208, 213–16, 231–3, 242. For his discussion of revelation in Liberalism, Yearley draws especially on Newman's 'On the Introduction of Rationalistic Principles into Revealed Religion', *Ess.*, 1: 30–101. This work originally appeared in 1836 as Tract 73.
74. See Yearley, *The Ideas of Newman*, 111. See *Ess.*, 1: 194–5; 69–70; 80–2; 82–3.

75. John Hick, especially, understands Jesus' significance in terms of God's 'Agapé'. See Hick's *Metaphor of God Incarnate*, 76–7; *God and the Universe of Faiths* (London: Macmillan, 1973), 153–63.

76. In his co-called 'biglietto speech', upon becoming a Cardinal in 1879, Newman described Liberalism as the 'one great mischief' to which he had 'opposed' himself throughout his career. See *Campaign*, 394–5.

77. For a discussion of the character of Liberalism, see my 'Newman's Catholic Synthesis', *Irish Theological Quarterly* 60 (1994) 39–48.

78. For this evolution, see Paul Knitter, 'Toward a Liberation Theology of Religions', *The Myth of Christian Uniqueness*, 178–97.

79. For a discussion of this point and the reference to Cupitt's view, expressed in a seminar discussion, see Brian Hebbelthwaite, 'John Hick and the Question of Truth in Religion', *God, Truth and Reality*, 124–34, especially p. 130.

80. *Ari.*, 80.

81. *GA*, 110.

82. Karl Barth, *Church Dogmatics*, vol. 3: 4 (Edinburgh: T. & T. Clark, 1961) 479, quoted in Avery Dulles, *Models of Revelation* (Garden City, N.Y.: Image Books) 10.

83. See David Tracy, *Plurality and Ambiguity: Hermeneutics, Religion and Hope* (San Francisco: Harper & Row, 1987) 90.

84. Regarding Newman's phenomenological approach, see, for example *PN*, 1: 127–39. See Yearley, *The Ideas of Newman*, 4–9, 20, 35–7.

85. *GA*, 263.

86. *Dev.*, 86: 'Revelation consists in the manifestation of the Invisible Divine Power, or in the substitution of the voice of a Lawgiver for the voice of conscience'. See also *US*, 172; *PS*, 8: 204–5.

87. *US*, 117–18; *PS*, 1: 320–4; 2: 18–19; *Apo.*, 46; *Ari.*, 84–5; *GA*, 420.

88. *GA*, 392.

89. *US*, 117. See also *GA*, 400, 395, 416. Newman offers a number of explanations of the insufficiency of conscience and, by extension, of natural religion. On a number of occasions, spread throughout his life, he ascribes it to conscience's lack of a sanction, beyond itself, for its elevated claims about the Moral Governor and Judge (*Mir.*, 19–20; *US*, 26–7; *OS*, 66; *Idea*, 515–16; *LD*, 27: 54–5; *Diff.*, 2: 253–4; *DA*, 133; *Ari.*, 80–1). These are therefore prey to societal pressures and to the individual's own inclination to abandon the moral ideal as impracticable (*US*, 23; *Mir.*, 19; *Diff.*, 2: 253–4; *Idea*, 515–16; *PS*, 2: 103; *HS*, 3: 79–81). In an early University sermon, (and it would seem, again in the *Grammar*), Newman maintains that it is, above all, the obscurity of the object of one's religious instincts and aspirations, that is, the dearth of information about God's 'personality', which saps one's moral resolve and raises the spectre of the futility of the moral and religious enterprise (*US*, 26–7; *SN*, 302; *GA*, 118). In the *Grammar* and, to some extent, in the *Parochial and Plain Sermons* and in *The Arians of the Fourth Century*, it is the sense of one's culpability and one's inadequacy to the moral task which exposes natural religion's inherent insufficiency (*GA*, 487; *PS*, 2: 155; *Ari.*, 146; *LD*, 27: 55). In all three cases, Newman proposes that the only adequate complement to the essentially incomplete natural religion of man is 'revealed' religion, which is to say, 'the doctrine taught in the Mosaic and Christian dispensation, and contained in the Holy Scriptures', which does not supplant, but builds on, nature's authentic teaching (*Ari.*, 79). See also *US*, 24, 115–18, 242–50; *Ess.*, 1: 22; *PS*, 1: 320–4; 2: 18–19; *Apo.*, 46.

90. *GA*, 118.

91. *GA*, 420, 409, 418. See also *Ari.*, 84–5.

Notes on Contributors

CYRIL BARRETT, SJ, was formerly Reader in Philosophy at Warwick University and is now a Tutor at Campion Hall, Oxford. He is the editor of Wittgenstein's *Lectures and Conversations on Aesthetics, Ethics and Religious Belief* (1966) and author of *Wittgenstein on Ethics and Religious Belief* (1992).

RONALD BEGLEY is an assistant professor of Classics at St Michael's College, Vermont, USA.

AVERY DULLES, SJ, is Lawrence J. McGinley Professor of Religion and Society at Fordham University, New York, USA. His books include: *Apologetics and the Biblical Christ* (1963), *The Survival of Dogma* (1971), *Models of the Church* (1974), *Models of Revelation* (1983), *The Catholicity of the Church* (1985), *The Reshaping of Catholicism* (1988), *The Craft of Theology: From Symbol to System* (1992), *The Assurance of Things Hoped For: A Theology of Christian Faith* (1994).

SHERIDAN GILLEY is Reader in Theology at Durham University. He is the author of *Newman and His Age* (1990) and co-editor of *A History of Religion in Britain* (1994).

IAN KER is a Tutor at Campion Hall and a member of the Theology faculty at Oxford University. His books include: the Oxford critical editions of *The Idea of a University* (1976) and *An Essay in Aid of a Grammar of Assent* (1985), *John Henry Newman: A Biography* (1988), *The Achievement of John Henry Newman* (1990), *Newman on Being a Christian* (1990), *Newman and the Fullness of Christianity* (1993), *Healing the Wound of Humanity: The Spirituality of John Henry Newman* (1993).

JOHN MACQUARRIE was Lady Margaret Professor of Divinity at Oxford. His books include: *Principles of Christian Theology* (1966), *God-Talk* (1970), *Existentialism* (1972), *Paths in*

Spirituality (1972), *The Faith of the People of God* (1972), *In Search of Humanity* (1982), *In Search of Deity* (1984), *Twentieth-Century Religious Thought* (1988), *Jesus Christ in Modern Thought* (1990), *Mary for All Christians* (1990).

TERRENCE MERRIGAN is a professor of Theology at the Catholic University of Leuven, Belgium. He is the author of *Clear Heads and Holy Hearts: The Religious and Theological Ideas of John Henry Newman* (1990).

AIDAN NICHOLS, OP, is a member of the Divinity faculty at Cambridge University. His books include: *The Art of God Incarnate: Theology and Image in Christian Tradition* (1980), *The Theology of Joseph Ratzinger: An Introductory Study* (1988), *Yves Congar* (1989), *Theology in the Russian Diaspora: Church, Fathers, Eucharist in Nikolai Afanas'ev (1893–1966)* (1989), *From Newman to Congar: The Idea of Doctrinal Development from the Victorians to the Second Vatican Council* (1990), *The Shape of Catholic Theology: An Introduction to its Sources, Principles and History* (1991), *A Grammar of Consent: The Existence of God in Christian Tradition* (1991), *Rome and the Eastern Churches: A Study in Schism* (1992), *The Panther and the Hind. A Theological History of Anglicanism* (1993), *Byzantine Gospel: Maximus the Confessor in Modern Scholarship* (1993), *Scribe of the Kingdom: Essays on Theology and Culture* (1994).

Index